THE COLOURS OF
LONDON BUSES

1970s

First published in Great Britain in 2016 by
Pen & Sword Transport
an imprint of
Pen & Sword Books Ltd,
47 Church Street,
Barnsley,
South Yorkshire,
S70 2AS

A CIP record for this book is available from the British Library.

ISBN 978 1 47383 777 5

The right of Kevin McCormack, to be identified as the author of this work has been asserted by him in accordance with the Copyright, Designs and Patents Act 1988.

Printed and bound in India by Replika Press Pvt. Ltd.

Pen & Sword Books Ltd incorporates the Imprints of Pen & Sword Aviation, Pen & Sword Maritime, Pen & Sword Military, Wharncliffe Local History, Pen & Sword Select, Pen & Sword Military Classics and Leo Cooper.

For a complete list of Pen & Sword titles, please contact
Pen & Sword Books Limited
47 Church Street, Barnsley, South Yorkshire, S70 2AS, England
e-mail: enquiries@pen-and-sword.co.uk
website: www.pen-and-sword.co.uk

Title page: The photographer displays his artistic bent in this view of Tilling ST 922 in Park Lane, passing Hyde Park, in Summer 1972. This veteran vehicle, with well-filled upper deck, is working Vintage route 100. *(Bob Greenaway/Online Transport Archive)*

Rear cover: Travelling along Top Dartford Road, near Hextable, on its journey from Chelsfield via Orpington, St Mary Cray and Swanley to Dartford on route 477, hired Eastbourne Borough Council AEC Regent V No 68 undergoes a sea change (!) to more inland surroundings on 24 January 1976. *(Charles Firminger)*

Front cover: In a contrast of colour, RML 2280 races RM 643 to Trafalgar Square as both buses exit Whitehall on 21 April 1973. The Hanimax livery only lasted for seven months, after which RML 2280 advertised Myson's for just over two years before reverting to red livery. *(Bob Greenaway/Online Transport Archive)*

THE COLOURS OF
LONDON BUSES

1970s

by Kevin McCormack

PEN & SWORD
TRANSPORT

The author, holding his 14-month-old daughter, Laura, poses precariously at the route 87 terminus in Abbey Wood Lane, Rainham, in September 1978.

Introduction

The 1970s was the first decade in London's history where, following the creation of London Transport (LT) in 1933 and the removal of the independent operators from the streets, buses and coaches were not necessarily painted in the traditional mainly red or green liveries. A Routemaster appeared in 1961 in unpainted aluminium (the so-called 'Silver Lady') as an experiment but was soon painted red. A sign of the future, however, appeared at the end of 1969, with the painting of the first London bus in all-over advertising livery, presaging a new trend for advertisers to promote their products by colouring vehicles (sometimes garishly) and emblazoning them with pictures and slogans. However, the use of these vehicles was controlled (normally only one per route at a time) so that red livery always predominated. The same control was exercised when commemorative liveries were applied for limited periods, for example, celebrating HM The Queen's Silver Jubilee in 1977 or Shillibeer's first London omnibus service (1979). All-over advertising continued into the early 1980s. The break-up of LT and subsequent privatisation largely brought it to a halt, but created a different problem – operators on franchised routes running buses in their own livery, sometimes with no red in evidence. Operators were then compelled to have their fleets at least 80 per cent red to maintain the Central London tradition expected by tourists and other visitors. With the introduction of the new Routemaster, some all-over advertising has been re-introduced.

A departure from traditional Central Area red or Country Area green also occurred during the 1970s, as a result of an acute shortage of operational buses for LT services and those services handed over on 1 January 1970 to newly formed London Country Bus Services (LCBS), a subsidiary of the National Bus Company (NBC). The shortfall was filled by the temporary use of other operators' vehicles in their own liveries. A number of buses in 'vintage' London livery could also be found on the streets during the 1970s.

The pictures in this colour album appear in strict date order and, as the title suggests, the book concentrates on the 1970s. However, as a precursor to that decade the first few photographs, which have a connection with the 1970s, date from the 1960s and the final picture in the book is a tongue-in-cheek look at the 1980s. Most of the images were taken in Central London but, for added variety, there is some material taken in the suburbs and the nearby country area, the yardstick being to keep within, or, very occasionally, just outside the M25 orbital motorway.

While there are a few of my own photographs included, this book would not have materialised had I not been able to use the work of other photographers. The vast majority of pictures have been supplied by the Online Transport Archive, a charity set up to preserve transport films and photographs. A recent collection which has been donated to the Archive comprises photographs taken by Bob Greenaway, an employee of LT who tragically died young. It has been a pleasure to present his excellent work to a wider audience in this way. Those photographs credited to Roger Harrison and Chares Firminger are supplied courtesy of Robert Bridger who holds the originals. As far as is known, none of the pictures appearing in this book has ever been published before.

The text is based on information from a variety of sources, but I must mention in particular two excellent web sites, Ian's Bus Stop (maintained by Ian Smith) for vehicle histories and Ian Armstrong's Bus Routes.

We are fortunate that a large number of the types of London bus featured in this book have been preserved in working order, either owned privately or by the two major public museums focussing exclusively on London public transport vehicles: the London Transport Museum at Covent Garden and Acton and the London Bus Museum in Cobham Hall, Brooklands. It is therefore still possible to ride on examples of these wonderful machines at museum events, garage open days and local running days.

Kevin R McCormack, Ashtead, Surrey
November 2014

Whereas it is the 1970s, which are normally associated with different coloured London buses, a unique departure from LT Central Area red livery occurred in the early 1960s, when the 'Silver Lady' (RM 664) entered service in July 1961 in unpainted aluminium (except for the fibreglass parts such as the bonnet which were painted silver). Other operators were also trying out this idea because it was thought that economies could be achieved by eliminating expenditure on painting and also reducing running costs through the consequent weight reduction. LT had adopted this approach for some of its Underground stock so, theoretically, it should have been successful for buses but, as this picture near Hyde Park Corner illustrates, the aluminium finish quickly became shabby, not helped by the use of washing plants. In addition, there was concern that as buses often required the fitting of replacement panels following bodywork damage, unpainted vehicles would lack a uniform appearance. RM 664 moved between eleven garages to gauge opinion but the experiment was abandoned after four years, the bus being painted red in August 1965. This view dates from March 1964, during the vehicle's two month stay at Cricklewood garage, and depicts RM 664 pursuing RF 120 on a 705 Green Line working. The body of RM 664 was subsequently fitted to RM 577, which has been preserved, although it has not proved practicable to return it to its unpainted aluminium condition. (Jim Jordan/Online Transport Archive)

Unlike RT family vehicles (numbering almost 7,000 LT buses in total), which were fitted with bodies built by several manufacturers, all 2,760 LT Routemasters, except two of the four prototypes, carried Park Royal bodies. This view at the Park Royal Vehicles factory in West London dates from Summer 1965 and depicts four identifiable brand new long Routemasters (RMLs). From left to right, these are Nos 2298, 2294, 2297 and 2296. All except RML 2294 spent their first few weeks of operational life on loan to the Country Area at Godstone, to fill a gap caused by the delayed delivery of green RMLs. All four continued in London service for almost forty years until 2004/5 whereupon they were sold, RML 2298 going to Germany, RML 2294 to Long Beach, California, RML 2297 to Italy and RML 2296 to a buyer nearer to home (Colchester Arts Centre). The photographer seems to have gained access to Park Royal Vehicles' premises, unlike the author who had to make do with poking his camera lens through the wire fence bordering the adjacent canal bank! *(Bob Greenaway/Online Transport Archive)*

With several operators purchasing front-entrance, rear-engine buses in the early 1960s, LT ordered eight Park Royal-bodied Daimler Fleetlines (classified XF) for evaluation purposes in the Country Area to compare with fifty Leyland Atlanteans (classified XA) trialled in the Central Area. Legislation now allowed larger capacity single deckers to be used for one-person operation (OPO), but not yet double deckers. The intention was for the XAs and XFs to be operated as dual purpose vehicles, conductors being employed in peak periods with both decks open, but with the top deck blocked off at other times for OPO, until such time as the double deck restriction ceased. The XFs were found to outperform the XAs but in case that was because Country Area operation was less demanding, the classes were exchanged on two occasions, resulting in the green XFs operating in Central London where they still outperformed the XAs! This photograph depicts brand new XF3 at Park Royal Vehicles' premises around August 1965, prior to its entry into service at East Grinstead on 15 September 1965. The XFs passed to LCBS in 1970 and, on its withdrawal in December 1981, XF3 became the last former LT-owned bus in the fleet. The vehicle was then bought for preservation, along with XF1, the remaining six being scrapped. *(Bob Greenaway/Online Transport Archive)*

This is a view of Park Royal Vehicles' yard on 15 June 1966, with brand new Sheffield Corporation buses on the left and in the distance the unique front-entrance, rear-engine Routemaster, FRM 1, which was to become a victim of circumstances. To set the scene, Park Royal Vehicles had been a well established independent commercial body builder for many years but in 1949 it was taken over by Associated Commercial Vehicles (ACV) which already controlled a number of subsidiaries including AEC. In 1962, the ACV Group merged with Leyland Motors which produced its own front-entrance, rear-engine double decker, the Atlantean, and saw the development of the FRM as a threat. In the end, only one FRM was built, being delivered to LT in the same month as this picture was taken. FRM 1 then underwent a year of trials before entering service in June 1967. The bus, which incorporated some eighty percent of standard Routemaster parts, was well received both by crews and passengers and, had circumstances and timing been different, a large fleet could have been built. This may have averted the misfortunes which plagued LT during the 1970s as a result of the decision to cancel the FRM project and purchase inferior OPO vehicles unable to withstand London's demanding traffic conditions or fit into LT's engineering regime. *(Bob Greenaway/Online Transport Archive)*

The Regent Low Height (RLH) class of Weymann-bodied provincial-style vehicles was introduced in 1950, more by luck than judgement. LT needed to replace its mixed and aging fleet of lowbridge buses and learned that Midland General, having ordered thirty such AEC Regent III buses, actually only needed ten! LT took the remaining twenty, liked them and ordered a further fifty-six. Most of the class were painted green for use in the Country Area, but the remainder were red for the four Central Area lowbridge routes, which operated from Merton (127), Dalston (178) Harrow Weald (230) and Hornchurch (248). The last of these to be introduced was the 178 in May 1959, mainly using surplus RLHs following the abandonment of the 127 in August 1958. Route 178 was the last RLH-operated service, succumbing in April 1971, and this evening shot depicts a resplendent RLH 53 at Clapton Pond on 24 September 1966. This bus, which entered service at Harrow Weald garage for route 230 in November 1952, was withdrawn in September 1970 and exported to the USA. It was repatriated, along with RLHs 69 and 71, in April 2012 and currently resides unrestored in the London Bus Museum at Brooklands, acting as the 'Regent Cinema'. *(Alan Murray-Rust/Online Transport Archive)*

British European Airways (BEA) was formed in 1946 and contracted with LT for the latter to operate coach services for passengers between Central London and the London airports. Initially, BEA's London flights were mostly based at Northolt but once the Central Terminal Area at Heathrow opened in late 1954, BEA transferred all its London flights to Heathrow. At first Commer Commando one and a half deck coaches were used on the coach services but when larger vehicles were needed (as the size of aircraft grew), BEA ordered sixty-five stylish 8 foot wide new coaches based on the Regal IV chassis with Park Royal bodies. These were also one and a half deck coaches with the rear seats raised to accommodate a large luggage compartment beneath but, unlike the Commers, they had a level roof line with no 'hump'. When the Regal IVs were introduced between April 1952 and May 1953, BEA was operating from the Central Air Terminal at Waterloo, on part of the former 1951 Festival of Britain site, but this was replaced in 1957 by a new West London Air Terminal at Gloucester Road, convenient for Heathrow, which was built on a concrete raft across the Cromwell Curve Underground junction. Withdrawn in 1966/7 (except for one, see page 26), these airline coaches normally travelled along the A4 Bath Road to and from Heathrow, but in their last few months of service they used the M4, the relevant section opening in 1965, and this shot is taken on the M4 Airport Spur. *(Bob Greenaway/Online Transport Archive)*

LT's operation of the airport service on behalf of BEA involved driving the vehicles, garaging them and maintaining them. The Regal IVs were selected because, mechanically, they were comparable with LT's fleet of RFs. It therefore came as no surprise that, when larger vehicles were needed as aircraft had again increased in size and the Regal IVs were past their prime, the replacement buses were Routemasters. In 1964, LT had trialled the unique forward entrance extended Routemaster, RMF 1254, on these services towing a luggage trailer. The experiment was successful, apart from the combined length of the bus and trailer being regarded as excessive, and consequently sixty-five replacement vehicles, also with forward entrances, were built, albeit to the standard length. Despite the BEA Routemasters being short, the passenger capacity of fifty-six still exceeded that of the Regal IVs by nineteen seats. With the opening of the London end of the M4, it was possible to reduce journey times significantly and these Routemasters were modified to allow them to hurtle down the M4 at around 70mph hauling their luggage trailers. This photograph shows one travelling at speed on the M4 and was taken on the same day as the previous picture during the period when the Regal IVs were being superseded. (*Bob Greenaway/Online Transport Archive*)

AEC were known as the Builders of London buses from 1912-1979. The origins of the famous company, killed off by British Leyland in 1979, began with Arthur Salisbury Jones who set up the Motor Omnibus Company Ltd, trading as Vanguard, and started assembling buses at Blackhorse Lane, Walthamstow, in 1906. His business merged with the large London General Omnibus Company (LGOC) in 1908, with bus building continuing at Walthamstow, as it did when the Underground Group took over LGOC in 1912. The group immediately decided to split bus operations and bus manufacturing, setting up The Associated Equipment Company (AEC) to handle the latter business on the same site. AEC subsequently moved from Walthamstow to new premises in Windmill Lane, Southall, in 1927, where this picture was taken on 9 July 1967. The buses seen here are brand new RMLs 2672 and 2680, which have recently arrived as complete vehicles from Park Royal Vehicles for final pre-delivery checks, etc. Interestingly, RML 2672 is carrying the registration number NML 672E, but all RMs after RML 2657 were registered with the later F suffix and RML 2672's number was changed to SMK 672F. The reason for the change was because the RMLs immediately following 2657 did not enter service until September 1967, when the F suffix was in use for new vehicles. (Bob Greenaway/Online Transport Archive)

Although overall advertising on London buses is synonymous with the 1970s, the phenomenon started in late 1969 and continued on a more limited scale into the 1980s and even up to the present day. The pioneer was RM 1737, advertising Silexine Paints. This vehicle, which had originally entered service in November 1963, was painted in the colours shown here (no stick-on vinyls in the 1960s/70s) at Aldenham Works in July 1969 and, following a launch ceremony, was put to work on route 11 and based at Riverside garage, Hammersmith. With its subtle shades, this livery is generally regarded as one of the most attractive examples of overall advertising, but the bus was only in these colours for thirteen months, after which it was repainted red. Withdrawal came in April 1985 and as it had latterly been a cosseted garage 'Showbus' and was in particularly good condition, it was chosen to represent the Routemaster class in the LT Museum at Covent Garden although, with body changes on overhauls, the present RM 1737 is not the same one that carried Silexine Paints livery. This photograph, taken on 16 August 1969, shows the vehicle turning from Duncannon Street into the Strand, opposite Charing Cross station. The building behind the bus is a section of the triangular block of shops and offices designed by Nash and built between 1830 and 1832, which still stands today. (Bob Greenaway/Online Transport Archive)

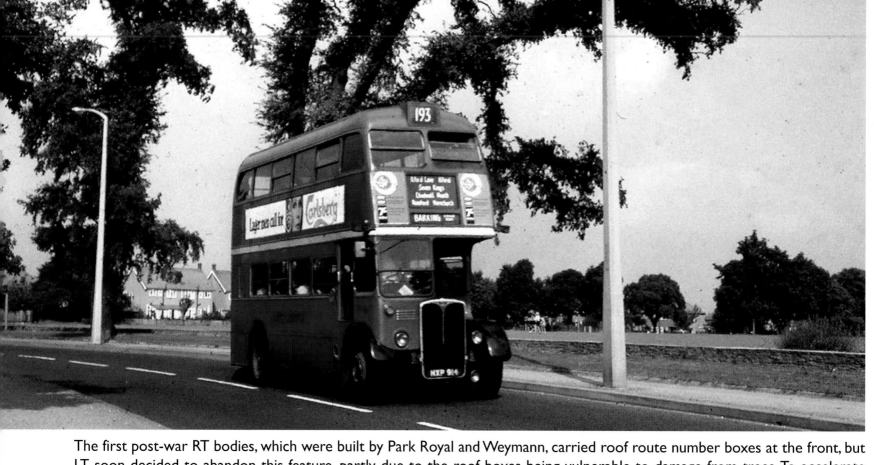

The first post-war RT bodies, which were built by Park Royal and Weymann, carried roof route number boxes at the front, but LT soon decided to abandon this feature, partly due to the roof boxes being vulnerable to damage from trees. To accelerate the introduction of RTs to replace the aging bus fleet, LT also went to two other body builders, Cravens and Saunders, but it was too late to change the specification to eliminate roof boxes so both builders included them. The Cravens RTs were so non-standard that they were prematurely withdrawn and sold off, but the Saunders RTs were retained, becoming the last vehicles in service with roof boxes. When it came to reducing the RT fleet, the Saunders RTs were on the hit list because they were still somewhat non-standard and obtaining certain body parts was becoming difficult. Consequently, when saloon heaters started to be fitted to RTs, the Saunders vehicles were not so treated (except one, apparently by accident) in anticipation of their earlier withdrawal. For most, this came on 13 June 1970 when all remaining RTs without saloon heaters and in public use were withdrawn. Hornchurch garage's RT 4661, seen here on 6 September 1969, had entered service in January 1954 with a Park Royal non-roofbox body and acquired its Saunders body on overhaul in October 1965. It was sold for scrap in October 1970. *(Bob Greenaway/Online Transport Archive)*

An infiltrator lurks at the back of Plumstead garage among the RTs and Merlins on 8 February 1970. This is Metro-Cammell-Weymann (MCW) Metro-Scania Demonstrator reg no VWD 451H, which LT hired in November 1969. The vehicle was trialled at Plumstead on route 99 from February-May 1970, after which LT ordered six of this single deck type. The Demonstrator was returned to MCW but was subsequently hired by LCBS in July 1971 for use at Stevenage, prompting that company to acquire seven. The other identifiable buses in the picture are RT 4384 and MB 626. The RT entered service in September 1953 and was transferred to Plumstead garage following overhaul at Aldenham in October 1969, when it received a body change. It was sold for scrap in March 1975. MB 626, a single door fifty-seater AEC Merlin designed for OPO suburban work, entered service in August 1969 and was withdrawn in June 1976, whereupon it was sold for further use and not scrapped until 1987. *(Bob Greenaway/Online Transport Archive)*

Mention has already been made on page 9 of the Park Royal-bodied Leyland Atlanteans (XA class), which were trialled against the XFs, the latter being regarded as superior. These types also ran comparison tests with RMLs, which were found to be better still. Following completion of the various trials between 1965 and 1969, the fifty-strong XA fleet was removed from Central London routes and shunted out to less demanding work in the suburbs. Six XAs were dispatched to Peckham garage to operate on a new circular OPO route (the P3) around Peckham and Nunhead, which was introduced on 24 January 1970, replacing route 173. Their reign, however, was rather short because route P3 was converted to single deck operation using AEC Swifts on 17 February 1973, whereupon the XAs were taken out of service. All fifty members of the class were then sold to the China Motor Bus Company of Hong Kong where they remained in service until 1980. This photograph depicts XA 32 on 8 February 1970 in Peckham Rye (the road) near the junction with Nunhead Crescent. (Bob Greenaway/Online Transport Archive)

The photographer did not have to travel far to take this picture – just across his bedroom to the window! Turnham Green-based MBS 265 is heading along Popes Lane in Ealing, near the junction with Knight's Avenue (opposite), on its way from Chiswick to Greenford Red Lion on route E3. This was one of the three Ealing routes converted to OPO on 30 November 1968 – a sad day because another of the casualties was the author's local RT-operated route 97, which became the E2. MBS 265 entered service in November 1968 for use on the E3 and was one of the two-door Central Area suburban standee Merlin buses built by AEC with MCW bodywork. Thirty-six foot long, they originally had accommodation for twenty-five seated passengers and forty-eight standing, but seating was almost immediately increased to thirty-two. MBS 265 was withdrawn in August 1975 after a typically short LT service life for these vehicles and exported to Mauritius in 1977. (Bob Greenaway/Online Transport Archive)

Seemingly pursued by wild horses (but they are actually pulling a carriage!), RM 1611 passes the Portland stone façade of The Park Lane Hotel, opposite Green Park in Piccadilly on 25 May 1970. The hotel was built by the property developer and hotelier, Sir Bracewell Smith in 1927 on the site of some Georgian houses and is Grade II listed. RM 1611 entered service in June 1963 and was withdrawn in July 1984. It then operated in Scotland for Stagecoach and Magicbus until withdrawn once more and exported to Missouri, USA, in 1996. The bus is taking part in the Festival of London Stores, a parade which was inaugurated in 1968 when it was attended by Princess Alexandra and her family, and which was intended to promote British exports and tourism. The parade generated a dispute in the House of Commons in the following year because, unlike in 1968, it was not allowed to start in Hyde Park on the grounds that it was too commercial to justify the use of a Royal Park. *(Bob Greenaway/Online Transport Archive)*

What better sight than a gleaming RT and hard to believe that it is twenty years old! Repainted at Aldenham in May 1970, the bus is seen at the former Staines West station terminus in the following month. Unfortunately, its magnificence was short-lived and does beg the question whether it was worthwhile overhauling this particular vehicle. It was only given a two-year Certificate of Fitness, which was not extended, and consequently it was withdrawn in April 1972 and scrapped. Route 225 did not fare much better either. Introduced on 20 March 1965 as a Mon-Fri peak hours replacement for the West Drayton – Staines West railway service, this route was operated by Uxbridge garage and required just two RTs, but was withdrawn on 16 January 1971, and partly covered by a re-routeing of the 224. Behind RT 4009 is RF 507, which also features on page 44 and was fortunate to escape scrapping. *(Online Transport Archive)*

The 248 was one of the four Central Area routes that required the use of the lowbridge RLH class of provincial-looking Regent IIIs. These buses had replaced the Leyland Tiger (TD class) single deckers in February 1955, albeit only four were initially required as it was a very short route (just over 2 miles at its longest, but most journeys (Upminster Station – Cranham) covered a distance of little over 1 mile). The RLHs were almost 1 foot lower in height than an RT, yet had almost the same seating capacity (fifty-three as opposed to fifty-six passengers). With the maximum length for buses being restricted to 30 foot long in the early 1950s, the RLH provided a means of avoiding the use of additional single deckers (with a maximum of forty-one seats) and extra crews on the busier routes where an offending bridge was only a little too low for an RT. Of course, once length limitations were relaxed, it was possible to use OPO long single deckers such as the AEC Swifts, this being the solution adopted for replacing the RLHs, which operated the 248 for the last time on 18 September 1970. This view of RLH 68 shows the vehicle passing under the low bridge, which is in St Mary's Lane, Cranham. Double deckers are now used on the 248, which has been extended beyond Upminster to Hornchurch and Romford, and re-routed away from the low bridge. *(Bob Greenaway/Online Transport Archive)*

RLH 71 proceeds along St Mary's Lane, Upminster, to the Hall Lane extension of route 248 on 15 August 1970. When the seventy-six vehicles of the RLH class entered service between May 1950 and December 1952, Nos 1-52 were in green livery for the Country Area and 53-76 were red for the Central Area. The twenty-four red examples were subsequently augmented by a further seven repainted from red to green over their years of service. Following withdrawal in 1971, RLH 71 went to America in early 1972 where it remained until repatriated in April 2012 along with RLHs 53 and 69. Many RLHs were exported at the end of their working lives to represent red London buses, because their reduced height gave them more operational flexibility, given the random height of bridges overseas. However, the majority of Londoners, finding these abroad, would not be familiar with a red bus having a sunken upstairs gangway and transverse bench seats, which required passengers sitting beside an upstairs window, to virtually have to climb over any fellow passengers on the same seat to extricate themselves. It would also be necessary for the fare and the ticket, together with any change, to be passed to and from the conductor via the other passengers. *(Bob Greenaway/Online Transport Archive)*

Against a somewhat Dickensian backdrop, RM 971 makes its way from Shepherd's Bush to Liverpool Street along Lillie Road, Fulham, on 21 April 1971. The bus is wearing the first version of the Yellow Pages livery, which it had just received. The vehicle entered service at Stonebridge Park in January 1962 on trolleybus replacement services but was working from Dalston garage when pictured here. RM971 was repainted into red livery in April 1973 but had a relatively short working life, being withdrawn at Enfield garage in September 1982 and broken up at Aldenham in March 1983. Route 11 is famous for being one of the oldest still operating, having been introduced in August 1906, and is widely regarded as an economical option for sightseeing, since it passes several famous landmarks. From 29 January 1994, route 11 ceased to serve Lillie Road, after being cut back from Hammersmith to its present western terminus at Fulham Broadway, which followed an earlier abandonment of the Shepherd's Bush – Hammersmith section. (*Bob Greenaway/Online Transport Archive*)

At the Bus of Yesteryear Rally at Waterloo (near today's London Eye) on 23 May 1971, an example of the ill-fated 'Londoner' type double decker bus, DMS 114, was displayed alongside the LT Museum's STL 469 to show how bus design had developed over nearly forty years. The DMS portrays the economic, but boring, Central Area livery of the time, relieved only by the short-lived open roundel on the side. The STL wears its final service livery, with white relief band but no relief around the windows. DMS 114 had just entered service at Stockwell but quickly moved to Wandsworth where it remained until withdrawal and scrapping in March 1979. STL 469 was one of 400 of the class with 'leaning back' bodies, entering service at Chalk Farm in July 1934. This veteran spent the final two months of its career as a red bus at a Country Area garage (Dartford) where it was withdrawn in January 1954 before joining the LT Museum's collection, which was then stored in Reigate garage. (Bob Greenaway/Online Transport Archive)

These airline coaches, all but one of which are Routemasters, are lined up at the West London Air Terminal at Gloucester Road on 15 July 1971. They are wearing BEA's final 'trendy' livery of tangerine and white and carry the airline's last logo, introduced in 1968. Furthest from the camera is BEA's last one and a half deck Regal IV coach, MLL 740, the only example from the original fleet of sixty-five to survive in service long enough to receive these colours. Apart from one scrapped earlier following a crash, the remainder of the class were withdrawn in 1966/7 as the sixty-five replacement forward-entrance Routemasters with luggage trailers were delivered. MLL 740 was kept as a spare vehicle and remained in intermittent service until withdrawal in May 1973, whereupon it was bought privately for preservation and is currently displayed at the London Bus Museum, Brooklands. LT bought four from BEA to use as mobile uniform issuing units, with the vehicles becoming changing rooms (with blanked out windows) and the uniforms carried in a trailer, these lasting until 1976/7. *(Bob Greenaway/Online Transport Archive)*

Here is DMS 114 again (see page 25), something of a coincidence given that there were 2,646 members of the class! Orders were placed for these Daimler Fleetlines as a result of the relative success of the trials involving the XF class, and bodies were split between Park Royal Vehicles and MCW. Route 170 (Wandsworth – Aldwych), a bus replacement for tram service 31, was converted from RT to DMS OPO operation on 24 July 1971, about the time when this photograph at Charing Cross station in the Strand was taken. In the background on the left are the famous 'pepper pots' of Coutts Bank dating from 1830-2, whose beauty is in stark contrast with the block on the right, Villiers House, built in 1957-9. The obelisk on the extreme right is the replica Eleanor Cross erected by the South Eastern Railway in 1865 to enhance the forecourt of its new station and hotel. The original cross in the hamlet of Charing was one of twelve erected in 1291-94 to mark the stopping places between Lincoln and Westminster Abbey of the body of Queen Eleanor, wife of King Edward I. The cross originally stood at the top of Whitehall but was destroyed in 1647 and replaced by the equestrian statue of Charles I in 1675, which still stands today. (Bob Jones/Online Transport Archive)

27

Newly painted RML 2702 from Upton Park garage lays over in Telford Road at the Ladbroke Road terminus of route 15 from East Ham on 31 July 1971. The Eagle public house (250 Ladbroke Road) remains in business and the Penfold hexagonal pillar box, a Victorian design from the 1866-79 period, is still standing. Even RML 2702 survives today, in the fleet of Geldards Coaches, Leeds, who acquired it following withdrawal in September 2004. What is more, route 15 is the sole service on which 'old' Routemasters still operate, albeit only five of them, and they are confined to the heritage route section (Tower Hill – Trafalgar Square). For the route as a whole, full OPO conversion from RMLs occurred on 30 August 2003 and the heritage operation commenced on 12 November 2005. RML 2702 entered service in October 1967 at Hanwell garage (the former trolleybus depot) and remained there until painted into all-over advertising for Homepride Flour in July 1971. The livery is dominated by their cartoon character, Fred the flour grader, who celebrated his fiftieth birthday in 2014. However, images of Fred did not adorn RML 2702 for long – the bus was repainted red three months later! *(Bob Greenaway/Online Transport Archive)*

This is a 65 service at Chessington Zoo on 16 June 1972 and RT 1706 is not on fire but is illuminated by a mid-summer sunset! The vehicle entered service in April 1950 and was withdrawn and sold for scrap in 1978. Route 65, operating between Ealing (Argyle Road) and Leatherhead, was introduced in December 1924 and the 1925 edition of the LGOC's bus map gives a journey time of 116 minutes, with via points at the southern end listed as Chessington Common, Ashtead Common and Leatherhead Common. There is no mention of Chessington Zoo as this did not open to the public until 1931 (and is still open today as part of Chessington World of Adventures). The scheduled time for the full route had reduced to 94 minutes by the 1950s but this was still one of LT's longest routes and, because there was nowhere at or near the Argyle Road terminus (actually in Cleveland Road) for the crew to obtain refreshments (there were toilets in Cleveland Park but no café), a mobile staff canteen was provided from Southall garage. The 65 now operates only between Kingston and Ealing Broadway which would be of no help to the author's friend who travelled daily on the 65 to school in Eaton Rise (north of Ealing Broadway) from his home in Hook. To make this journey now would not be viable because it would involve using three bus services. *(Bob Greenaway/Online Transport Archive)*

The pigeons in Trafalgar Square have now been banished but Tilling ST 922 still turns a wheel today, albeit not operating a daily bus route in Central London but in well-earned retirement at the London Bus Museum, Brooklands. This busy scene dates from 23 June 1972 and ST 922 is working on Vintage Bus route 100, operated by Obsolete Fleet Ltd. This service ran for some ten years with different routeings but almost entirely using ST 922, which proved to be extraordinarily reliable. The route had various sponsors over the years including, at the time of this photograph, Johnny Walker, the whisky brand. The bus is waiting at the traffic lights on the eastern side of Trafalgar Square, heading for Whitehall. The Routemaster on the right is standing at the western end of the Strand, having passed Charing Cross station. Trafalgar Square's fountains were installed to limit the amount of space available for public demonstrations although this expedient has had only limited effect over the years! *(Bob Greenaway/Online Transport Archive)*

One of the less garish bus liveries on the London streets in the 1970s was that advertising Uniparts as carried by RM 249 between May 1972 and May 1973. The vehicle entered service at West Ham in March 1960 and worked from Mortlake garage on route 9 during its all-over advertising period. Route 9 has been dubbed one of London's oldest existing bus routes, having been introduced in 1908. This service ceased to be crew-operated when Routemaster operation was withdrawn on 4 September 2004, only to become crew-operated again when the new Routemasters ('Borismasters') were introduced on 26 October 2013. In the meantime, a 'heritage' section of route 9 with traditional RMs was introduced on 14 November 2005 but was withdrawn on 25 July 2014, ostensibly due to lack of patronage. RM 249 became surplus to requirements with the onset of OPO and was withdrawn in September 1985 and sold for scrap. In this photograph, taken in the Strand on 23 June 1972, it is being overtaken by another London icon, a black FX4 cab. These taxis originated under the Austin marque in 1958 and production continued under various names until 1997. *(Bob Greenaway/Online Transport Archive)*

Here is an opportunity to study Uniparts RM 249 in more detail as it leads a convoy of Routemasters towards Charing Cross station in the Strand, again on 23 June 1972. The production models from RM 5 to RM 253 were built with non-opening upper-deck front windows, but RM 249 now has a later body with opening windows. In fact, the vehicle had four body changes during some twenty-five years of service, these occurring in January 1964, August 1970, January 1977 and August 1981. Other alterations made to this vehicle following its construction include the removal of the brake ventilator grilles below the headlights (brakes were found not to overheat) and the heater ventilator grilles above the cab and canopy. On RM 249, only the lower section has been plated over (some RMs had the top half covered over as well, allowing the flake grey cant rail relief band to be continuous). The vehicle also has the revised form of radiator grille. On the left of the picture is the Nash-designed Coutts Bank building with its eastern end 'pepper pots'. This frontage is much improved in appearance today following the replacement of the motley collection of ground floor retail establishments with more aesthetically pleasing shop fronts, which are recessed and stand behind columns, being visually separated from the offices above by ornate iron railings. *(Bob Greenaway/Online Transport Archive)*

A trio of very different looking London buses make their way along Whitehall towards the mounted sentries at Horseguards on 23 June 1972. Nearest the camera is an East Kent Guy Arab III dating from 1951 on hire to LT for the Round London Sightseeing Tour which, shortly after its return to East Kent, became a towing vehicle. Standing alongside the Guy Arab is RM 967 operating out of New Cross on route 53 (Plumstead – Camden Town). This vehicle entered service in November 1961 and was sold to a private buyer following withdrawal in 2003. It currently resides in Scotland. An unidentified RT follows up the rear. The buildings seen here stand on the western side of Whitehall and the portico in the centre of the picture behind the buses belongs to Dover House, a Grade I listed building, which houses the Government's Scotland Office. Dover House was built in 1758 and the portico was added in 1788. *(Bob Greenaway/Online Transport Archive)*

Ignore the 'pepper pots', it's time to concentrate on beer! On 28 June 1972, RML 2701 veers across the Strand in its Tartan livery advertising Youngers beer, pursued by a Truman beer lorry. The bus entered service at Hanwell in October 1967 and carried Youngers livery from May 1972 until August 1973. It was withdrawn in March 2004 and is now owned by RM Buses Ltd of Wigan who hire it out for special events. Unlike RML 2701, the beer lorry is unlikely to still be working, but Truman, once the world's largest brewer, made a come back in 2013 after a twenty-four year absence, beer once more being brewed in East London, close to the original brewery in Brick Lane where production began as long ago as 1666. The main casualty in this view seems to be the Midland Bank. Following its creation in 1836, the bank underwent various name changes, settling on 'Midland Bank' in 1923. This famous name remained on our streets until 1999 when rebranding took place following acquisition by HSBC in 1992. *(Bob Greenaway/Online Transport Archive)*

Lions watch over Trafalgar Square as LCBS's RT 940 passes by on the southern side on 28 June 1972. Whereas green buses/coaches in central London were usually those operating Green Line services, training vehicles also appeared in order that learner bus drivers could become accustomed to dense traffic conditions and large numbers of pedestrians. RT 940 entered service as a red bus at Potters Bar in December 1948 and became green on overhaul in September 1963, whereupon it went to Hemel Hempstead. Soon after its transfer to LCBS on 1 January 1970, it became a trainer at Dartford for nearly five years until sold for scrap in March 1976. The four bronze lions that guard Nelson's Column were sculpted by Sir Edwin Landseer and are said to have been cast from the cannons of French and Spanish vessels defeated by Britain at the Battle of Trafalgar in 1805. Although part of the original design for the square, the lions were not put in place until 1867, sixty-two years after Nelson died. *(Bob Greenaway/Online Transport Archive)*

Here is an apology for a green London bus, RML 2547, advertising the bookmakers, Ladbrokes. Entering service at Hackney in September 1966 for route 6, it remained at Hackney through to the end of 1972, which included most of its time in Ladbrokes colours, this lasting from June 1972 to February 1973. Withdrawn at Willesden in March 2004, the bus, now engineless, is at the time of writing (November 2014) up for sale by London Bus and Truck Ltd of Northfleet. The photograph was taken at Piccadilly Circus on 28 June 1972 and immediately behind the bus are the offices of the former County Fire Office Insurance Company (50 Regent Street), built in 1924-7 and replacing a similar looking County Fire Office, which was demolished in 1924. To the right is the former Regent Palace Hotel whose distinctive façade and some internal features have been retained following demolition and reconstruction as offices in 2010-12. The area around the intersection of roads at this point was regarded as a particularly fashionable and exclusive part of London in the seventeenth century and the name, Piccadilly, is said to be derived from 'pickadill', which was a type of stiff collar of that period. (Bob Greenaway/Online Transport Archive)

In order to trial the concept of introducing open top buses for its 'Round London Sightseeing Tour', LT hired some East Kent Park Royal-bodied Guy Arabs in 1972 (see page 33), FFN 380 being caught on camera in Knightsbridge on 30 June 1972. This bus was one of a batch of forty highbridge fifty-six-seat double deckers ordered by the East Kent Road Car Company in 1951, some of which were converted in the late 1960s to open toppers for Kent coastal routes and painted in a reversal of that company's traditional livery where maroon predominated over cream. The conversion seemed to age these buses, giving them something of a pre-war appearance, but they were an attractive addition to the capital's streets and had not succumbed to National Bus Company (NBC) corporate livery, NBC having absorbed East Kent into its organisation. The buses were crewed by East Kent drivers and LT conductors during their one summer of service in London and this vehicle, after being converted to a tree-lopper on its return to East Kent, was sold for scrap in August 1976. *(Bob Greenaway/Online Transport Archive)*

We remain in Knightsbridge on 30 June 1972 and witness a cycling hippy averting his gaze from the garish sight of the ice cream parlour, which is masquerading as RM 2140. This bus entered service at Bow in February 1965 and worked from Battersea garage during its stint on route 22 as an advertising vehicle for Bertorelli ice cream. This service from Putney Common to Homerton has a claim to fame because it was the one on which RT 1 made its public operational debut on 9 August 1939, marking the start of RT day-to-day working in London, which lasted until 7 April 1979. RT 1, now belonging to the London Bus Museum, made forays on route 22 during 2014 to celebrate the seventy-fifth Anniversary of the RT bus. RT 1 was taken off route 22 in March 1940 and the service returned to being exclusively STL operated, which remained the position until RTWs took over in 1951. These were replaced in 1966 by RTLs (and RMs on Sundays), the RTLs being superseded by RTs in 1967 but only for a month before complete conversion to RM operation occurred. Extended Routemasters (RMLs) took over Monday to Saturday services in 1987 and this continued until 22 July 2005 when they were replaced by OPO double deckers. Meanwhile, RM 2140 had been withdrawn from New Cross back in March 1987 and sold for scrap. (*Bob Greenaway/Online Transport Archive*)

8 April 1972 was the launch date for LT's Vintage Route 100, which saw ex-Tilling ST 922 gracing the streets of London in almost daily operation for some ten years. This AEC Regent 1 entered service in November 1930 for Thomas Tilling, and was one of 191 such vehicles taken into LT stock following the ousting of the independent operators from LT's traffic area. The bus was withdrawn in 1939 but put to non-public use at Tunbridge Wells, then loaned to a Birmingham operator from December 1941 to November 1944 and returned to London service until being withdrawn again in December 1946. It was then converted to a mobile staff canteen, becoming No 693J, and ending its days at Belmont. Upon withdrawal, this veteran was bought by British Road Services for continued use as a canteen at their Tufnell Park depot, before ending up in a scrapyard near Hitchin where it became a store. Prince Marshall, who had kept an eye on it for many years, was able to buy it in 1965 and have it rebuilt. In this view in Summer 1972, ST 922 has just pulled off the stand in Horse Guards Avenue. The neo-gothic building behind the bus is the National Liberal Club, completed in 1887 and the statue in the foreground is that of Spencer Compton Cavendish (1833-1908), Eighth Earl of Devonshire, a former leader of the Liberal Party. (Bob Jones/Online Transport Archive)

ST 922 is now entering Whitehall, heading towards Trafalgar Square, once it has negotiated the equestrian statue of Prince George, Duke of Cambridge (1819-1904), who was Commander-in-Chief of the British Army from 1856 to 1895. Behind the bus is the Old War Office Building, a neo-Baroque structure built during 1901-6. The Routemaster on the extreme left is about to stop outside 55 Whitehall, built in 1909 for the Commissioners of Woods and Forests and now occupied by the Department of Energy and Climate Change. ST 922 is carrying pre-war Central Area livery with a silver-painted roof. In order to make vehicles less visible to enemy aircraft during the Second World War, roofs were painted brown and subsequently red following the introduction of the simpler early post-war livery for buses (trolleybuses retained brown roofs to conceal oil splashes from the overhead equipment). *(Bob Jones/Online Transport Archive)*

These two buses, RT 2278 and RM 21, are standing on the east side of Whitehall, opposite the Horseguards mounted sentries, in Summer 1972. The building partly obscured by trees behind the RT is the Banqueting House, the only part of the Palace of Whitehall to survive (the remainder, comprising King Henry VIII's Tudor palace, having burnt down in 1698). The Banqueting House is Grade I listed and a fine example of Palladian architecture. It was designed by Inigo Jones and built in 1619-22 for King James I with the intention that the palace would be rebuilt in similar style, but this plan never came to fruition. The building in the background to the left is the former War Office. RT 2278 entered service at Mortlake in July 1949 and was withdrawn from Bexleyheath in November 1976, being sold for scrap. It is working here from Elmers End garage on a short working of Route 12 (Harlesden – South Croydon). RTs and RTLs took over this service completely in November 1949 and full conversion from RT to RM operation occurred on 12 May 1973. RM 21 entered service at West Ham in November 1959 and was withdrawn at New Cross in August 1984 and also sold for scrap. Route 53 (Camden Town – Plumstead Common) lost its RMs in favour of Scania double deckers (MD class) on 8 January 1977. *(Bob Jones/Online Transport Archive)*

Travelling along Camden Road, Holloway, RM 686 looks to be carrying a full load as it works a short southbound journey to Mornington Crescent station on route 29 (Southgate – Victoria) on 29 August 1972. All the buildings in this shot are still extant, the tall building on the right being the Castle Bar, 392 Camden Road, currently a guest house. RM 686 entered service at Edmonton in April 1961 and had just gained Vernons all-over advertising livery when seen here, a livery which it retained until September 1974. It was withdrawn from Muswell Hill in March 1986 and sold for scrap. Route 29 underwent complete conversion from RT to RM operation on 22 March 1969 although the London Underground strikes of 2014 did bring RTs back, running shorts from Holloway (Nags Head) to Trafalgar Square. The route flirted with crew-operated DMs (Mon-Sat) and Metrobuses (Sun) during the mid-1970s and mid-1980s, before reverting to RM operation. Full conversion to OPO working was introduced on 5 November 1988. *(Bob Greenaway/Online Transport Archive)*

RM 787, seen here at Finsbury Park on 29 August 1972, has had, and continues to have, an interesting life. Entering service at the former trolleybus depot at Stamford Hill in July 1961, the vehicle remained there for sixteen years before changing garages, and ended its London operational life at New Cross, being withdrawn in January 2005. In the previous October it had lost its original registration number, WLT 787, and took a new number, 792 UXA. Following withdrawal, RM 787 was sold to Ensigns and converted to open top. The vehicle is now owned by the York Pullman Bus Company and is available for wedding hire. In this view, the bus is working a 253 service (normally Aldgate – Tottenham Court Road), which was introduced on 1 February 1961 to replace trolleybus route 653. The 253 remained a Routemaster operation until OPO buses were introduced on 21 November 1987. (Bob Greenaway/Online Transport Archive)

The 700-strong RF class of AEC Regal IVs with Metro-Cammell bodywork were the mainstay of LT's single deck fleet during the 50s, 60s and much of the 70s, owing their longevity to the fact that they were excellent vehicles and superior to the buses that were meant to replace them. This example, RF 507, entered service at Sidcup in March 1953 and from May 1972 to July 1977 was based at Croydon garage. This view depicts it in Woodcote Road, Wallington, working a 234A service (Hackbridge – Purley Old Lodge Lane) on 29 August 1972. This route was introduced on 3 August 1938 and was RF-operated from 12 January 1953 to 29 January 1977, with OPO being introduced on 7 August 1966. The RFs were replaced by BLs, which were themselves superseded by Leyland Nationals in 1982, but the route was withdrawn two years later. RF 507 subsequently moved to Kingston and has a claim to fame through operating the very last scheduled RF service on 30 March 1979 (into the early hours of 31 March!). Following withdrawal, the bus spent some five years with an Army Cadet Unit at Waltham Abbey before being purchased for preservation in 1984. *(Bob Greenaway/Online Transport Archive)*

Having travelled from north London to Surrey on 29 August 1972, the photographer has found the unique front-entrance, rear-engined OPO Routemaster, FRM 1, described on page 10. Entering service at Tottenham in June 1967, disaster struck two months later when it caught fire and firemen had to smash some windows (none of which were designed for opening) to release smoke. Following repairs and the fitting of some openable windows, FRM 1 returned to Tottenham where it remained until August 1969, moving in December 1969 to Croydon for route 233, a single bus requirement. When this route was converted to Swift operation in March 1971, FRM 1 was transferred to route 234, working alongside XAs, and is operating this service when pictured here in London Road, Hackbridge. With the replacement of the XAs by DMSs in January 1973, FRM 1 was transferred to Potters Bar for another route requiring a single bus, the 284, operating this service from October 1973 until September 1976, when it incurred accident damage. Following repairs, it was fitted out for use on the Round London Sightseeing Tour, operating from January 1978 until its withdrawal in February 1983, whereupon it was handed to the LT Museum for preservation. *(Bob Greenaway/Online Transport Archive)*

This is a bus which has had a very interesting life: experimental LT livery, fruit and vegetable shop, playbus and preservation! This two-door flat fare AEC Metro-Cammell-bodied Merlin, MBA 588, entered service at Walworth for Red Arrow services in January 1969. In August 1972, the vehicle was painted in an experimental red and white livery and was the first bus to sport the large white LT roundel. Entering service at Gillingham Street (Victoria) in the following month, it was clearly in newly painted condition when photographed on 21 September 1972 on the south side of Lambeth Bridge in front of the rather austere Lambeth Bridge House, a Government building dating from 1941, which has been replaced by very futuristic-looking 'luxury' apartments. MBA 588 reverted to standard livery in March 1976 and was withdrawn at Walworth in June 1981. It was then purchased by Feltham Community Association and ended up being used as a static grocery shop. When it was no longer required, it was sold and became a pub garden play bus in Sussex. After serving in these ignominious roles, MBA was purchased privately for preservation and moved to its present home at the Wythall Transport Museum, Worcestershire, on 20 February 2002. (Bob Greenaway/Online Transport Archive)

There are a number of candidates for the most garish livery on a London bus and this is one of them: RM 1270 advertising Sharp car radios at Hyde Park Corner on 23 September 1972. This bus entered service at Mortlake in December 1962 and received Sharp Electronics livery in May 1972, following which the vehicle was sent to Clapton for use on route 22, retaining these colours until January 1974. The scrapman beckoned following its withdrawal at Enfield in February 1987. The magnificent backdrop to the picture consists of, on the left, the Grand Entrance to Hyde Park designed by Decimus Burton and constructed in 1825 and, behind the bus, Apsley House. This building dates originally from 1771-8 and was designed by Adams for Lord Apsley, the Lord Chancellor. It was the first building reached by visitors from the countryside passing through the tollgates in Knightsbridge and became known as Number 1, London (but now, more prosaically, 149 Piccadilly!). The Duke of Wellington subsequently purchased Apsley House and commissioned Wyatt to design improvements. These included having the original brick exterior clad in Bath stone and adding the pedimented portico in 1829, which is how this Grade I listed building looks today. (Bob Greenaway/Online Transport Archive)

There is a dearth of passengers on this Green Line coach, symptomatic of the downturn in patronage suffered by Green Line in the 1970s. In this view in Park Lane on 23 September 1972, St Albans garage have turned out RF 178 in a respectable condition for this 713 service, but no wooden roofboards are carried. RF 178 entered service at Dorking in March 1952 and was one of 175 Green Line coaches to be modernised in the mid-1960s, by which time the original coaches were beginning to look dated, having been introduced in 1951. Route 713 ran from Dorking to Dunstable via Victoria (some summer journeys went to Whipsnade Zoo) and was converted to OPO on 15 February 1969. On 31 May 1975, the route was officially shortened to operate only between Victoria and St Albans, a practice increasingly adopted for Green Line services in order to avoid the cross-London congestion, which caused so much late running. However, shortening the route failed to save it and it was axed on 28 January 1977. Meanwhile, RF 178 was withdrawn in January 1975. *(Bob Greenaway/Online Transport Archive)*

Staines garage must have been desperately short of vehicles for Green Line services on 23 September 1972 because they have produced, not even an un-modernised coach, but a country bus. RF 594, seen here passing the former Duke of Wellington's home (see page 47) at Hyde Park Corner, is working a short to Victoria instead of operating the whole 701 route from Ascot to Gravesend. This routeing of the 701 service ran for the last time on 3 October 1975, only for a new 701 to start operating from 20 May 1978 between Victoria and Windsor with a summer extension to the former Safari Park (now Legoland) and travelling non-stop between Hammersmith and Heathrow using the M4. RF 594 entered service at Windsor in June 1953 and was withdrawn from that garage in March 1973. However, it was destined to have an extended life, being converted by LCBS into a recruiting office, a role it performed until final withdrawal in October 1980. Green Line service 701 still runs past this spot (Victoria – Bracknell via Windsor and Ascot) operated by First. *(Bob Greenaway/Online Transport Archive)*

Sunglasses are required (or blindfolds!) for viewing this picture taken in Park Lane on 23 September 1972. With the bus painted in such gaudy colours, this hardly looks like a Red Arrow service, which may account for the apparent absence of passengers and why it very quickly had at least the front repainted red! The vehicle in question is AEC Merlin MBA 606, which entered service in September 1969 at Gillingham Street, Victoria, for these limited stop routes. It received this, the first version of all-over Chappell's livery, in the same month that this photograph was taken, and went on to receive a second version in July 1974. Returning to red livery in July 1975, MBA 606 was withdrawn in May 1981 and sold for scrap. There were many problems with the Merlin class, not least their length, which at thirty-six feet made them difficult to turn, thereby stressing their bodies, and the tendency for their engines and gearboxes to overheat as a result of constant stop-starting due to heavy traffic and bus stops being close together. However, enthusiasts saw a silver lining in this: had it not been for the unreliability of the Merlins and their shorter cousins, the Swifts, as well as the Fleetlines, RTs and RFs would not have lasted until 1979! (Bob Greenaway/Online Transport Archive)

Hardly a London bus, but LT had a large service vehicle fleet to support its bus and underground operations. This vehicle, 1273LD, was the first of a batch of eight Leyland PD3A/1s used as railway breakdown tenders and entered stock on 13 December 1962. The body was built by Mann Egerton of Norwich and mounted on a bus chassis, providing a low height platform to facilitate the loading and unloading of heavy equipment. One was normally stationed outside Baker Street station, as indeed this one was at the start of its service life, but when this picture was taken on 28 January 1973, it was allocated to the Permanent Way Engineer's Department at Lillie Bridge Underground depot and kept at Stockwell bus garage. The vehicle, despite being only ten years old, is looking well past its prime in this picture, but remained in stock until delicenced at Lillie Bridge on 5 September 1978, and subsequently sold. In this view, 1273LD is standing at Kew Gardens station while the bridge carrying the District Line and North London Line over Mortlake Road (the A 205 South Circular Road) was being repaired. One of these breakdown tenders, 1279LD, has been preserved. *(Bob Greenaway/Online Transport Archive)*

A livery arguably easier on the eye was that worn by RM 1740, seen here proceeding southwards along Park Lane, with the Marble Arch junction in the background, on 24 April 1973. This bus entered service at Cricklewood in November 1963 and was painted to advertise Danone in March 1973, carrying these colours for six months, whereupon it was repainted red. During the 1980s, RM 1740 joined the training fleet and was used as a skid bus at Chiswick Works before being withdrawn in July 1990 and exported to Uruguay where it was used by a radio station. Route 73 was introduced on 30 November 1914, running between King's Cross and Barnes. Over the last hundred years, the service has been extended and has contracted a few times. At the time this picture was taken the full route was Stoke Newington – Hammersmith, extended to Hounslow on Sundays. RMs were first introduced on the 73 on 5 December 1962 from Tottenham garage (where RM 1740 was based when photographed here) and fully converted on 3 October 1965. Routemaster operation lasted until notorious 'bendy buses' took over on 4 September 2004. *(Bob Greenaway/Online Transport Archive)*

The distinctive emblem of the *London Evening News*, as emblazoned on RML 2302, represented the setting sun, but within a few years the newspaper was itself to sink below the horizon. Founded in 1881 and acquired thirteen years later by the Harmsworth brothers, who were later to become Lord Northcliffe and Lord Rothermere of Associated Newspapers/*Daily Mail* fame, the *Evening News* was becoming unprofitable in the 1970s and merged with its rival, the *Evening Standard,* in 1980. Red RML 2302 entered service in October 1965 on a short term loan to Godstone, along with several others because not enough green RMLs had been delivered in September 1965 for the scheduled replacement of fifty-six-seater RTs by seventy-two-seater RMLs and a phased changeover was to be avoided (larger capacity buses normally meant fewer vehicles). The Country Area RMLs were ordered in two batches of fifty and there was no desire to upset the chronological number sequence of the green buses. *(Bob Greenaway/Online Transport Archive)*

The stopgap red RMLs were not required once further green ones had arrived at Godstone, so RML 2302 was able to take up Central Area duty at Stamford Hill in December 1965. The bus remained in red livery until October 1972 when it was painted to advertise the *Evening News* and moved between various garages (Upton Park, Chalk Farm, Putney and Hackney) during the ensuing twelve months or so, adding colour to several routes before being repainted red in November 1973. One of the interesting aspects of the all-over advertising craze of the 1970s was that some advertisers chose to have similar images on each side of the bus while others, such as the *Evening News,* adopted a more radical approach. As illustrated on this and the previous page, in these views taken in Fulham Road on 29 April 1973, the nearside of RML 2302 looked totally different from the offside. The Putney-based bus is operating on route 14 (Hornsey Rise to Putney (Kingston on Sundays)) and continued in service until withdrawal at Camberwell in November 2004, whereupon it was sold. *(Bob Greenaway/Online Transport Archive)*

Headless footballers chase after a ball, which has caused the RM fleet number to be transferred to the driver's door! Dismembered bodies painted beneath the lower deck windows so that passengers' heads would complete the image did not work when there was nobody downstairs, as evidenced by RM 762 at Stockwell on 29 April 1973, working route 2. The bus entered service at Edmonton in April 1961 and gained its all-over advertising livery for Esso Blue in November 1972, wearing these colours on routes operated by Holloway, Stockwell, Walworth and Willesden garages for a year before regaining red livery. The images and slogan on the side of the bus were designed to cash in on the popularity of Chelsea Football Club's recording (a Top 5 single in March 1972) called 'Blue is the colour, football is the game'. Route 2 has a claim to fame insofar as the prototype Routemaster, RM 1, made its public service debut on this service (Crystal Palace to Golders Green) on 2 February 1956. Route 2 was fully converted to Routemaster operation on 14 June 1967 and RMs were ousted following OPO conversion on 21 June 1986. RM 762 was broken up in 1993. (Bob Greenaway/Online Transport Archive)

This is another one for football fans! We are still in Stockwell on 29 April 1973 as Dorking's RF 166 crosses Landsdowne Way on its long journey from Dorking to Dunstable via Victoria on Green Line route 712. The building behind the RF, Wingfield House, advertising Banqueting Rooms (261 South Lambeth Road), has an interesting history, not least because it had a football club named after it. Founded as the Wingfield House Football Club in 1888, this non-league side changed its name to Nunhead Football Club in 1904. The Club's high spot was in the 1926-7 season when it reached the second round of the FA Cup, however it ceased playing in 1941. After its football association ceased, Wingfield House became the Jersey Home for Working Lads in 1911 and looks very smart today, having been converted into flats. Green Line coach RF 166 entered service at Luton in March 1952 and was modernised in December 1966. The vehicle was converted to OPO in April 1968, withdrawn at Windsor garage in April 1976 and sold for scrap. In this view, it is wearing bus livery, with yellow replacing the light green band, and all evidence of the Green Line roofboard brackets has been removed. *(Bob Greenaway/Online Transport Archive)*

LCBS also climbed on the trendy all-over advertising bandwagon and painted RMC 1490 to promote London & Manchester Assurance in March 1973, not restoring green livery (by this time NBC leaf green) until April 1977. This vehicle was one of sixty-eight 'short' Routemaster fifty-seven-seater coaches built for Green Line services, but when this picture was taken at Kingston railway station in late April 1973 it had been relegated to bus work, operating at this time from Reigate garage on route 406 (Kingston – Redhill) in company with RT 4496. Entering service at Epping in October 1962, RMC 1490 was re-acquired by LT in June 1979 and painted red in December 1980. It has since been preserved, unlike RT 4496, which was withdrawn in May 1980 and sold for scrap. Route 406 was introduced by the East Surrey Traction Company as their S6 service in 1920, being renumbered 406 in 1924. It is now a red bus route operating between Kingston and Epsom. As for the insurance company, London & Manchester Assurance existed under that name from 1869 to 1998 when it was taken over by Friends Provident (now Friends Life). *(Author)*

With no trace of green, this burger bus has brought the once prestigious Green Line coach services to a new low. RP 46 was one of three members of this ninety-strong class of Park-Royal bodied AEC Reliances to be so treated (but RP 46 is generally regarded as the most offensive) and this view dating from 29 April 1973 sees the coach negotiating the roundabout at Hounslow West, having travelled along the Great West Road on its journey from Sevenoaks to Windsor via Victoria on the now defunct 705 service. RP coaches had replaced the long Routemaster coach RCLs on 25 March 1972 as these were no longer regarded as projecting the right Green Line image to entice travellers away from cars and trains (though RP 46 would hardly help!), nor of course could the RCLs be converted to OPO which was now essential for maintaining Green Line services. RP 46 was new to Addlestone in January 1972 and carried Wimpey advertising from January 1973 to August 1976. The vehicle was withdrawn in December 1979 and is not one of the two class members known to have survived. (Bob Greenaway/Online Transport Archive)

Stockwell's RT 3949 enters Parliament Square from Parliament Street on 1 May 1973 on its way from Farringdon Street to Putney Heath on route 168. This service was introduced on 1 October 1950 as a replacement for tram route 26 and DM-type buses replaced RTs on Mondays-Fridays from 31 August 1975, having replaced RTs on Saturdays from March 1973. Subsequently, Routemasters took over until the route was withdrawn on 25 August 1981. RT 3949 entered service at Norwood in November 1950 and was withdrawn in March 1979, being sold for scrap. In November 1971, garages were ordered to remove the rear wheel discs, ostensibly on economy grounds (did they really take that long to remove and refit when changing a wheel?). The removal of the disc retaining brackets was sometimes less immediate and RT 3949 still has its in situ. The building in Bridge Street, behind the Merlin single decker, was demolished in 1994 to make way for new government offices known as Portcullis House, providing working accommodation for MPs. The grimy façade of the structure behind the RM and RT has received a deep clean since this picture was taken, one corner of which houses St Stephen's Tavern. (*Roger Harrison*)

This is the doyen of one of LT's least successful classes, the RC coaches. These were AEC Reliances with forty-nine-seat Willowbrook bodies but fortunately LT only ordered fourteen of them, these being delivered in November 1965. They presented a modern image for Green Line but were notoriously unreliable mechanically and spent much of their short working lives in store, all going for scrap upon withdrawal in 1978/9. LT seem to have been concerned about the longevity of these coaches from the outset because the prototype modernised RF, which had been commissioned in July 1965, emerged in March 1966, to be followed by a further 174 later in 1966 and 1967. Route 723 was one of the busy Aldgate bound services from Essex, which ran in direct competition with rail services and was operated in the 1950s and 1960s by double deck vehicles. RTs were superseded by more comfortable Routemaster coaches in July 1965, which in turn were replaced by OPO single deckers in January 1972. Official conversion took place using the more successful RP Reliance coaches, but Grays had a few RCs to supplement the RPs as evidenced by this view of RC1 at Aldgate on 13 May 1973. Behind the coach is the church with the full name of *St Botolph-without-Aldgate with Holy Trinity Minories*, a Grade 1 listed building dating from 1741-4 located at the junction of Houndsditch and Aldgate High Street. *(Bob Greenaway/Online Transport Archive)*

Still in Aldgate on 13 May 1973 the photographer has now found RM 783, which is wearing one of the all-over advertising liveries, which was more pleasing to the eye. The bus had entered service at Stamford Hill in July 1961 and acquired Esso Uniflow advertising livery in November 1972, followed by stints at Stamford Hill, Mortlake, Stockwell and New Cross, before being repainted red in January 1974. This picture was taken during its three-month stay at Mortlake and on this occasion it is working the short-lived Sundays-only 9A service. This route started on 9 April 1971 as a diversion from route 9 to serve the Tower of London, but various re-routeings of the 9 over the next few years saw this suffix number come and go until it finally vanished on 25 April 1981. RM 783 was to soldier on until February 1987 when it was withdrawn at Tottenham and sold for scrap. (Bob Greenaway/Online Transport Archive)

Throughout the 1970s, LT had to fall back onto the trusty RT class to substitute for more modern vehicles when the latter suffered from mechanical problems or there was a chronic shortage of spares. Route 40 (Poplar Blackwall Tunnel – Norwood Junction when this photograph was taken) was fully converted from RT to RM operation on 13 June 1970, so this view at Aldgate on 13 May 1973 shows Poplar's RT 1274 on RM substitution duty. Originally built with a Saunders roofbox body, this bus entered service at Leyton in December 1949 and was withdrawn at Seven Kings in May 1976, after which it was sold for scrap. RT 1274 did, however, enjoy a considerably longer life with LT than the bus behind, MB 182. This AEC Merlin entered service at Walworth as a Red Arrow standee, MBA 182, in September 1968 and was subsequently reclassified MB 182 following the provision of additional seating for suburban services. It was withdrawn in February 1975 (over a year earlier than RT 1275!) and was sold for further use, not reaching a scrap merchant until May 1980. This view depicts MB 182 working on route 42 (Aldgate – Camberwell Green) and, like RT 1275, appears to be substituting, in this case, for a DMS, this class having taken over from Merlins on 23 January 1973, which had themselves replaced RTs from 24 January 1970. *(Bob Greenaway/Online Transport Archive)*

LCBS made a bad decision when they started to place long Leyland National buses on some of their Green Line services, having gone to the effort of trying to impress potential passengers with the RP class of coaches. The LNC vehicles were not fitted with coach seats but with pvc-covered bus seats and no luggage racks were provided. LNC 59, seen here in Pall Mall on 1 June 1973, had only just entered service at Reigate in the previous month for use on Green Line service 711 (Reigate – High Wycombe) when the company realised its mistake and the LNCs were replaced on Green Line duties by shorter Nationals (SNCs) with coach seats. LNC 59 was put into store in February 1974 after being ousted from route 711 and was reclassified from a coach to a bus in February 1976, becoming LNB 59. Withdrawn in May 1984, the vehicle was sold for further service. Meanwhile, Route 711 had been discontinued from 1 October 1977. The building to the rear of the vehicle is Oceanic House, 1-1A Cockspur Street, a Grade II listed building built in 1903, which is shortly due to be converted into apartments. It was originally the London office of the Oceanic Steam Navigation Company, operator of the White Star Line, whose vessels included the ill-fated *Titanic*. (Bob Greenaway/Online Transport Archive)

1970s style traffic wardens dominate this photograph taken on 1 June 1973 at Oxford Circus. The subject of main interest, however, is RM 786 in all-over advertising livery for Ladbrokes, the bookmakers, with greyhounds featured on the nearside of the bus. Page 36 featured a more subdued version of Ladbrokes advertising on RML 2547 and at the same time as this bus was being restored to red livery in February 1973 so RM 786 was gaining this brighter version of Ladbrokes advertising which it carried up to November 1973 when it too was repainted red, having served at Hendon, Willesden and Battersea while promoting Ladbrokes. RM 786 had entered service at Stamford Hill in July 1961 and was withdrawn from Edmonton in April 1985, being sold for scrap. Route 8 (Old Ford – Neasden/Wembley) had been fully converted from RTW to RM operation on 1 February 1965, but is perhaps best known as the only route on which the third prototype Routemaster, RML 3, the unique Leyland bus with a Weymann body, operated. This took place between January 1958 and November 1959 and, excluding three months off the road following serious accident damage, resulted in a public service career of only some eighteen months. *(Bob Greenaway/Online Transport Archive)*

This military vehicle photographed in June 1973, is in fact, former Central Area RF 394. Entering service at Norbiton in January 1953, it operated out of various garages (mainly Sutton, Bromley, Edgware and finally Dalston), before being withdrawn in April 1971 without being converted to OPO, although it was fitted with doors during its LT service. In October 1971 the bus was acquired by D Company, 1st Cadet Battalion, King's Royal Rifle Corps (Putney). This cadet battalion was formed in the early 1890s and became part of the KRRC in 1894. In November 1979, the vehicle was sold to Purley High School for Boys (formerly Purley Grammar School for Boys), a school founded in 1914, which moved from Purley to Old Coulsdon in 1936 and closed in 1988. There is no published record of RF 394's life when it ceased to be a school bus, but the worst must be assumed as it does not appear on the long list of RF survivors. *(Bob Greenaway/Online Transport Archive)*

What today would be regarded as classic cars speed past Hendon's RM 682 on 28 June 1973 as the bus, on a route 13 short service, terminates at Aldwych behind a DMS on route 170. RM 682 entered service at Wood Green in April 1961 and received all-over advertising for Pye in May 1973, which it retained until December 1973 when it reverted to red livery. Withdrawn in November 1987 at Turnham Green, RM 682 was bought by Stagecoach United Counties and re-registered HVS 937 in 1992, its original registration, WLT 682, being transferred to a 1996 Volvo Olympian double decker. RM 682 was last recorded being used as a snack bar at an IKEA store in the Netherlands. Route 13 (at this time Golders Green – London Bridge) was converted from RT to RM operation on 18 December 1962 and fluctuated between partial and full Routemaster use until OPO Scania Omnidekka buses took over on 22 October 2005. As for route 170 (Wandsworth – Aldwych/Euston), OPO DMS vehicles replaced RTs on 24 July 1971. *(Bob Greenaway/Online Transport Archive)*

In contrast with the nearside of RM 786 featuring greyhounds (see page 64), the offside of this Ladbrokes advert bus was festooned with horses and jockeys. Pictured on 5 July 1973 at Marble Arch, the vehicle has just pulled out of Oxford Street and is about to negotiate the elongated roundabout at the end of Park Lane in order to reach Edgware Road on its journey from Old Ford to Willesden garage on route 8. It would seem that the arrival of this colourful bus may have taken the photographer by surprise as he has been unable to avoid street furniture appearing in his viewfinder. The present Marble Arch roundabout, much despised by cyclists due to motor vehicles jockeying for position, was created in the early 1960s when Park Lane was widened, leaving the historic Arch in effect stranded on a traffic island, although some effort has been made to improve its situation by the addition of a paved area and gardens. The seven-storey building on the left was erected in 1922 as a prestigious apartment block overlooking the Arch and Hyde Park and has since been converted to become the London Marriott Hotel, Park Lane. *(Bob Greenaway/Online Transport Archive)*

The largest operator of former LT buses in the 1970s, besides London Country, must have been Lesney Products, maker of Matchbox Toys. A large fleet of staff buses ferried workers from places such as Southend, Rochford and Benfleet to the factory in Hackney where this photograph was taken in Autumn 1973. The vehicles visible in this picture from left to right are ex-RTs 2700, 1260, 807, 3132, two unidentified ones, RT 3573, RF 650 and RTs 3150, 3154, 2938 and 3024. The company also had four RLHs and a few provincial buses. The dull blue livery seen here later gave way to brighter colours similar to those adopted by Stagecoach. Lesney Products was formed in 1947 by two unrelated school friends, Lesley Smith and Rodney Smith, taking the first and last three letters of their forenames. The company closed in 1982 following financial difficulties, and the Hackney factory has been demolished. (*Author*)

Stonebridge Park garage seemed to be a magnet for visiting training buses in the 1970s when the author worked about a mile away on the North Circular Road (the canteen may have been the attraction, given the distance these two buses have travelled). This view dating from Winter 1973 depicts London Country's RT 3751 from Luton garage and LT's RT 2502 from Camberwell, the former still retaining its LT radiator triangle (a Central Area one) despite the change in ownership and purge of LT 'bullseyes'. Like most RTs, both vehicles ended up on the scrapheap when they were withdrawn, neither finding buyers. Stonebridge Park had opened as a tram depot in 1906 and converted into a trolleybus depot in 1936. After becoming a bus garage in January 1962, it closed in August 1981. (*Author*)

Also at Marble Arch on 5 July 1973, RP 24 turns out of Oxford Street on a 715 Green Line service from Hertford to Guildford. This cross-London service, the first of its kind, was started in December 1929 by Mr Charles Dobb's Skylark Motor Coach Company and joined together two separate Skylark routes (Guildford – Oxford Circus and Oxford Circus – Hertford), which had been introduced in December 1928 and September 1929 respectively. Green Line Coaches Ltd, an LGOC subsidiary formed on 9 July 1930, commenced operations eight days later with a Charing Cross – Guildford service in partial competition with Skylark, which it actually acquired on 6 February 1932, the first of several rival operators taken over by Green Line in these early days. Route 715 (numbered as such from 6 February 1946, having originally been designated Route M from 4 October 1933) was the first to operate Routemaster coaches (RMCs) in August 1962, superseding RF coaches, and the Routemasters were replaced on the 715 by RPs in April 1972. RP 24 entered service at Romford in January 1972 and was withdrawn at Addlestone in March 1983, after being downgraded to a bus for many years. RP 21 and RP 90 have been preserved. (Bob Greenaway/Online Transport Archive)

We say goodbye to Marble Arch on 5 July 1973 with this view of probably the prettiest all-over advert bus, RM 294, which is promoting Celebrity Travel. At the time, this vehicle was based at Gillingham Street (Victoria) and working on route 137 (Crystal Palace – Archway). The bus is just entering Oxford Street and passing the Cumberland Hotel, a large edifice, which opened in 1933 on the site of an eighteenth-century inn, the *Duke of Cumberland*, named after King George II's son. RM 294 entered service at Highgate in November 1961 and carried Celebrity Travel advertising from April to September 1973. The bus was withdrawn at Enfield in December 1986 and sold for scrap. RMs replaced RTs and RTLs on route 137 on 1 November 1964 and Routemaster operation continued, albeit not exclusively, until the service was converted to OPO on 10 July 2004. *(Bob Greenaway/Online Transport Archive)*

This picture of Dalston-based MS 4 on route S2 taken on 2 September 1973 needs clarification on several fronts. Firstly, Metro-Scania single deckers were ordered by LT and LCBS at roughly the same time (see page 17 regarding the Demonstrator) and both organisations classified them MS, resulting in LT having MS 1-6 and London Country having MS 1-7, a recipe for confusion. Secondly, the small aperture for the blind display on the MS class was not ideal because the S2 was not a flat fare service from Clapton Pond to Bromley station in the London Borough of that name, but to Bromley-by-Bow station. Finally, the driver of MS 4, on its first day of operation (13 August 1973), took the other destination rather too literally and actually drove the bus, not just to the pond but into it! However, the bus quickly recovered from its wetting because here it is three weeks later. As a result of the problems with the Merlins and the Swifts, LT had ordered the six Metro-Scanias along with six Leyland Nationals (LNs) for comparison trials on the S2 with the intention of selecting a replacement type and settled for the LNs. The MS sextet remained on the S2 until withdrawal on 13 June 1976, whereupon they were put into store and sold, five going to Newport Corporation in Wales. MS 4 has since been preserved, along with MS 2. *(Bob Greenaway/Online Transport Archive)*

Flat-fare route S2 was introduced in April 1970, operating with MBS vehicles (Merlins) and replacing the RF-operated 208. In August 1973, the MBSs were joined by the six MS (Metro-Scania) buses and in the following November, the Merlins were replaced by the six LS (Leyland National) buses (see page 72). On 24 November 1973, LS 3 had an altercation with a van (the van came off worse!) and is seen here parked in Newick Road, opposite Clapton Pond, while LT staff review the situation and pigeons have a feast in the gutter. The MS and LS vehicles remained on the S2 until June 1976 when they were superseded by Swifts (SMS class) and the six LSs were transferred to Hounslow to join new class members there. The Swifts were then replaced by newer LSs on the S2 in November 1979. The route was eventually discontinued in July 2008. LS3 was withdrawn at Hounslow in June 1985 and sold for further use. *(Bob Greenaway/Online Transport Archive)*

This depressing scene is Stonebridge Park garage in Winter 1972/3, the only vehicle not in the doldrums being RT 4825 on the left. This was based at Shepherd's Bush from October 1965 to November 1978, latterly being used as a trainer, and was handed over to the LT Museum in February 1979 because it was numerically the last RT, although it was not, in fact, the final one built. Bodybuilders Park Royal and Weymann were allocated batches of numbers. Red RT 4825 was built by Park Royal and was completed in March 1954 whereas Weymann's last one was green RT 4794, delivered to LT on 11 November 1954, one day after their actual and numerical last RTL (1631). Indeed, as a result of the Aldenham Works overhaul programme this bus, numbered RT 4825, in fact consists of the chassis originally belonging to RT 1548 and the body built for RT 4600! Returning to the picture, the other identifiable upright buses are RT 688 and RF 316, which are both withdrawn and were sold for scrap in March 1973. Lying on its side is RT 4306, which became a practice turnover vehicle for training breakdown crews in September 1970 and allocated the service stock number 1602TV. *(Author)*

Another all-over advertising bus to have its fleet number moved to the driver's door was RM 952. This Dinky-liveried bus was popular, not only through being easy on the eye, but because the images depicted, though modern, were familiar to many and probably aroused feelings of nostalgia, particularly for transport enthusiasts. RM 952 entered service at New Cross in November 1961 and carried this livery between August 1973 and February 1975. It was withdrawn at Norwood in June 1986 and sold for scrap. This view shows the bus allocated to Streatham garage and it is working a 159 service (South Croydon garage/Thornton Heath – West Hampstead) on 7 March 1974. The vehicle is just emerging from Whitehall into Trafalgar Square, passing Drummonds Bank, 49 Charing Cross. The bank was founded in 1717 and became part of the Royal Bank of Scotland in 1924. The building was reconstructed in 1877-81 and is Grade II listed. On the right is Admiralty Arch, leading to Buckingham Palace. *(Bob Greenaway/Online Transport Archive)*

Following the creation of LCBS, the Company's first priority was to replace the crewed buses and coaches inherited from LT (mainly RTs, RFs and Routemaster buses and coaches) with new OPO vehicles. They chose to standardise on the basis of Leyland Atlanteans, in contrast with LT who had put their money on the Daimler Fleetlines. The double deck Atlanteans were classified AN but eventually there were several types designated AN, largely due to the acquisition of second-hand ones from different operators. AN 92, whose fleet number is almost hidden next to the garage plates, belonged to a batch (AN 91-120), bodied by MCW and entering service at Hertford in November 1972. On three occasions during its service life, it acquired all-over advertising livery, starting with the *Hertfordshire Mercury* whose newsprint was plastered over AN 92 from January 1974 to May 1976. In this picture, the bus is heading for Enfield on its journey from Hertford on route 310 and is making its way along Bullsmoor Lane, just past the junction with Langdale Gardens, on 16 March 1974. *(Bob Greenaway/Online Transport Archive)*

Nearly two weeks after being photographed leaving Whitehall for Trafalgar Square, RM 952 is back again (see page 75) but this time the nearside of the bus is on view, along with the opposite side of Whitehall. RM 952 still looks pleasantly eye-catching but instead of Dinky Toys on show, there is sample output from Meccano construction sets. As before, the bus is operating on route 159 (South Croydon – West Hampstead) and, as the destination shown is St John's Wood and not West Hampstead, this journey will not include travelling over the pedestrian crossing in Abbey Road made famous by the Beatles. The 159 ceased to operate north of Baker Street in 1992, replaced by new route 139, and was later cut back to Marble Arch. As regards the buildings in the background, the oldest is the one with four vertical columns behind the centre of the vehicle. This structure originally towered above those on either side when it was built in 1865 for the National Bank. (*Bob Greenaway/Online Transport Archive*)

You could wait ages in Oxford Street for an all-over advert bus to come along and then two arrive at the same time! The date is 20 April 1974 and Myson RML 2280 heads east to Oxford Circus as RM 1285 approaches in its livery promoting Peter Dominic wine shops. This bus entered service at Mortlake in December 1962 and publicised Peter Dominic from September 1973 to November 1974. It was withdrawn at Peckham in August 1982 and sold for scrap. In the background, on the extreme right, is Selfridges, the famous department store. This building was completed in three phases, in 1909, 1925 and 1929, the lack of continuity arising because of delays in the acquisition and demolition of existing buildings on the site. Oxford Street took its name because it was the main route westwards out of London. The fact that the Earl of Oxford purchased large amounts of land on the north side for development may also have influenced the decision to name it as such. Previously, the road had been called Tyburn Way as it led to the notorious public gallows near the site of Marble Arch. *(Bob Greenaway/Online Transport Archive)*

Here is a closer view of the Myson bus pictured on the previous page, RML 2280. In fact, the bus has been seen before, on the front cover, when it was advertising Hanimex Projectors. The bus carried this latter livery from March to November 1973 and was then immediately transformed into the colours shown here for Myson. RML 2280 had started life on loan to Godstone garage in the Country Area in August 1965 as one of the stop-gap newly delivered red RMLs to fill in for two months until new green RMLs arrived, whereupon the vehicle was transferred to Tottenham. Withdrawn at Clapton in October 2005, the bus was purchased by the Yorkshire coach company, Wilfreda Beehive. The equestrian statue to the left of the bus is of George IV and was erected on the east side plinth temporarily in 1844, pending its placement on top of Marble Arch. But that did not materialise, so it remains in Trafalgar Square. *(Bob Greenaway/Online Transport Archive)*

With its zebra stripes, this bus could be advertising London Zoo instead of sweets! Carrying one of the least 'easy on the eye' designs for all-over advertising, RM 906 pulls out of Whitehall into Trafalgar Square on a route 12 service to East Acton. The bus entered service in January 1962 at Finchley and carried this black and white livery for Barker & Dobson's Everton Mints from May 1973 to February 1975, being withdrawn in November 1991 and sold for scrap. Barker & Dobson were a husband and wife team (Dobson was the wife's maiden name) who opened a sweet shop in Liverpool in 1834 and whose business purchased the rights to a black and white humbug produced by 'Mother Noblett' for fans on their way to Everton Football Club's ground at Goodison Park. Everton FC started life as St Domingo's FC, which changed its name to Everton in 1879, at which point the renamed club's colours were black and white. Consequently, the humbugs with their black and white stripes and toffee centres were called Everton Mints, a brand still produced today. Barker & Dobson is now owned by Trebor Bassett and this group has now become part of Cadbury. *(Bob Greenaway/Online Transport Archive)*

You may think you have seen this bus before (on page 64) but you haven't! The livery is almost identical but now the radiator grill and headlamp surrounds are painted mauve – and it is a different vehicle. This is RML 2560 in Oxford Street on 20 April 1974 and a much travelled Routemaster at that. Entering service at Willesden in October 1966, it visited Montreal in Canada in March 1967 for Expo67 in company with RML 2548 where it became the Red Rose Tea Bus and had its side emblazoned with the slogan 'best bloomin' tea of the lot'. Not long after its return from Canada, RML 2560 was abroad again, this time to Esbjerg in Denmark, on a goodwill visit in April 1968. Back in Britain, the bus spent twelve months in Ladbrokes livery from October 1973 to October 1974 and remained in London service until sold in March 2004. The bus then crossed water yet again, but only as far as Northern Ireland, for it now travels around the Belfast area working for Allen's Tours. *(Bob Greenaway/Online Transport Archive)*

Aldenham Works at Elstree in Hertfordshire (close to Aldenham reservoir but some miles from Aldenham itself!) was once the most comprehensive bus overhaul 'factory' in the world. The huge 53-acre site was originally acquired by LT for the construction of a new Underground depot for the Northern Line in anticipation of a proposed extension from Edgware to Bushey Heath. However, completion of the facility in 1939 coincided with the outbreak of the Second World War, which caused the railway extension to be deferred. The introduction of Green Belt legislation after the war put paid to any significant housing development in the existing semi-rural locations to be served by the extension and LT abandoned the plans. During the war, the Aldenham buildings had been used as an aircraft factory for the construction of Halifax Bombers, following which LT decided to convert the buildings to create a bus repair and maintenance depot to supplement Chiswick Works, opening this new facility in 1949. By 1956, Aldenham had been developed into a major overhaul works for LT's entire bus and coach fleet (totalling around 8,000 vehicles at times), turning out rebuilt vehicles at the rate of some fifty a week on a three-year (later extended to four-year) cycle and employing nearly 2,000 people. This photograph and the following sequence were taken during a private visit on 21 May 1974, with this view depicting a Central Area Routemaster, and a BEA one receiving attention in the body shop. *(Bob Greenaway/Online Transport Archive)*

A Routemaster body shell submits to an underside steam clean after being rotated in Aldenham's inverting frame to remove road debris, etc. The body will then be picked up by a travelling crane and placed on raised stands for attention (see following picture). The concept of separating bodies from chassis and swopping these around was not an Aldenham initiative, but goes back over a hundred years to London's first mass-produced bus, the B type. However, the post-Routemaster generation of buses was not suited to this kind of dismantlement, which was liable to cause body distortion, resulting in the abandonment of body separation in the 1980s. This factor, coupled with the reduction in overhaul work arising from LT's Country Bus and Coach Department being hived off in 1970, helped to bring about the closure of Aldenham in November 1986. The buildings were eventually demolished in 1996 to make way for Elstree's *Centennial Park* business estate. *(Bob Greenaway/Online Transport Archive)*

The body shell of a long Routemaster (RML) is 'leapfrogged' over a line of RM bodies, having received some panel repair or replacement. From 1950 to 1956, Aldenham would remove the vehicle bodies for overhaul there, while the chassis were sent to Chiswick for overhaul. Once Aldenham was fully functioning as a major overhaul works in 1956, bodies and chassis/sub-frames were able to be renovated at Aldenham, with Chiswick dealing only with the running units. Body renovation took longer than chassis/sub-frame refurbishment, but LT was able to take advantage of its vehicle standardisation policy by swopping bodies and chassis so that no such delay occurred, achieving this by having a float of spare bodies. A further advantage was that licences could be fully utilised. With Ministry of Transport approval, LT was able to put back on the road a vehicle carrying the same fleet number and registration number as one which had arrived at Aldenham earlier the same day, even though it was a completely different bus! However, this historic concession understandably mystifies the current licencing authorities, thereby causing problems for subsequent preservationists trying to re-licence a vehicle which has been off the road for some time or wishing to reinstate an original registration number. *(Bob Greenaway/Online Transport Archive)*

A trolley jack lifts a dual-doored AEC Swift, which has received a re-paint after four years of existence (not necessarily four years of service, given their unreliability!). These buses, introduced from 1970, never received major overhauls at Aldenham although, after the expiry of their seven-year Certificates of Fitness, some received light overhauls in an effort to extract a further two years of life from them. All were withdrawn by 1981, having been largely replaced by Leyland Nationals. This photograph illustrates the bus's split entrance, the left-hand side taking the passenger to the driver and the right-hand side to an automatic fare machine. The intention was to speed up boarding on OPO buses but the machines often failed for reasons such as excessive vibration of the vehicle or running out of tickets, thus increasing rather than reducing delays. *(Bob Greenaway/Online Transport Archive)*

Four buses representing three generations of London bus stand at various stages of the overhaul process. From left to right, these are RML 2539, RT 2862, SMS 785 and RML 2619. Only two of these survive today, these being the RMLs. RML 2539, nearest the camera, entered service at Hackney in September 1966, was withdrawn at Camberwell in November 2004 and is preserved. RML 2619 began its service life at Holloway in May 1967 and ended it at Brixton in November 2005, whereupon it was also bought for preservation. RT 2862 entered service at Enfield in July 1952 and was withdrawn at Abbey Wood in December 1974 (so this overhaul seems to have extended its working life by only seven months) before being sold for scrap; while Swift SMS 785 was sold for scrap in August 1978, having entered service at Uxbridge in December 1971, therefore clocking up less than seven years of operational life. *(Bob Greenaway/Online Transport Archive)*

When LCBS took over LT's Country Area and Green Line coach services on 1 January 1970, the new company used Aldenham to overhaul its fleet until it opened its own engineering facility at Tinsley Green, near Gatwick, in 1976. Here we see MB 87 alongside DMS 1675 and RM 1312 and another RM, all three identifiable buses later having an 'after life'. Merlin MB 87 entered service at Reigate in March 1968 (so in LT days) and was sold by LCBS to Citybus, Belfast, in April 1980 and withdrawn in October 1981, followed by scrapping. DMS 1675 has just been delivered new and will shortly be sent to Chalk Farm. It was withdrawn in June 1982 and sold to Western Scottish, eventually being sold for scrap in January 1991. RM 1312 has had the most interesting life though. Entering service at Mortlake in December 1962, the bus was initially withdrawn in February 1994 and re-registered MFF 509, before being sold for preservation. Bought back for London service in September 2000, a time when sold-off Routemasters were being sourced from virtually anywhere, RM 1312 was withdrawn again in December 2005 and presented to Haags Bus Museum in the Netherlands. *(Bob Greenaway/Online Transport Archive)*

We have now entered the paint preparation area before the buses are put into the spray painting area for application of top coats. Considerable effort has been put into the refurbishment of this veteran, RT 3228, although the corner of the front nearside wing appears to still require attention. This bus belonged to a batch of thirty-six Green Line coaches (RTs 3224-3259) which were standard buses except for the addition of an external raised motif between decks and the absence of advertisements. RT 3228 spent most of its life in Green Line livery (and continues to!), having entered service at Romford in August 1950. However, on overhaul at Aldenham in April 1969, it became a red bus and was sent to Palmers Green and returned there following the overhaul taking place here. Withdrawn in March 1977, the vehicle was bought by a dealer and resold to Kingston Plant Hire Ltd. Acquired for preservation in 1980, RT 3228 entered Roger Wright's London Bus Company fleet in October 2008 and periodically operates services in connection with the Epping Ongar Railway. *(Bob Greenaway/Online Transport Archive)*

Also being prepared for final painting is an unidentified former BEA Routemaster, a member of this 65-strong class of forward-entrance vehicles. In terms of state-owned airline history, BOAC was formed in 1940 and BEA followed in 1946. Initially BEA relied upon BOAC to transport its passengers to and from Central London until it took responsibility in July 1947 for its own services and contracted with LT to operate them from March 1948. BOAC continued to run its own coach services from its airline terminal at Victoria right up to its absorption into British Airways (BA) on 1 April 1974. However, when BEA was absorbed on the same date the contract with LT remained and the Routemasters were painted into BA colours. The changeover from BEA's orange and white livery to BA's blue and white was not immediate and it is not clear into which livery the bus in the photograph is being repainted. The new paint around the headlights suggests ex-BEA orange but the amount of white paint points to BA livery. *(Bob Greenaway/Online Transport Archive)*

We are now in the spray paint bay and AEC Swift SMS 681 has all its external glass (windows, lights, blind boxes) masked for protection. The vehicle has received its top coat and some transfers and the final stage of the process will be varnishing. This particular OPO bus entered service at Potters Bar, replacing RTs on route 299 from 3 July 1971, and spent almost its entire operational life at Potters Bar, returning there from this repaint and being withdrawn at that garage in August 1980, followed by scrapping. The only other garage it worked from was Harrow Weald, for a few months in 1979. The AEC Swifts were purchased because the AEC Merlins were considered too long and unmanoeuvrable, as well as being unreliable. The Swifts were of a more practicable length, being some 2½ feet shorter at 33ft 5ins instead of 36ft. However, they were equally unreliable and, worse still, were significantly underpowered, with 8.2 litre engines compared with a Merlin's 11.3 litre (and an RT/RF engine size of 9.6 litres). (Bob Greenaway/Online Transport Archive)

RM 1206 demonstrates the tilt test which was the method used for checking the stability of new or modified vehicles. The platform beneath the bus was tilted by a hydraulic ram of 1.25 tons pressure and the requirements for a double decker was that it should be able to tilt to 28 per cent without turning over, ensuring therefore that the bus would be safe, for example, turning sharp corners. In fact, engineers would test the vehicle up to 38 per cent (just short of the 40 per cent limit), as illustrated here by the side dial. The bus had to have all its wheels standing on the ground to pass the test and it was not secured in any way, although, as seen here, there were rubber buffers to catch the vehicle if it tipped. Some two tons of sandbags would be strapped to the upper deck to represent thirty 10-stone passengers. The side dial shown here measured the chassis's angle of tilt. In some official photographs, there is also a front dial and this would measure the body tilt which would be influenced by the effectiveness of the springing. (Bob Greenaway/Online Transport Archive)

Instead of sandbags, RM 1206 has real people on board in the Tilt Test Shed, holding on very tightly! The angle of tilt is clearly considerable, judging by the building in the background, and the photographer has done well not to have fallen over. RM 1206 entered service at Norbiton in May 1962, later moving to Hounslow, back to Norbiton and then to Hanwell. It was withdrawn at West Ham in August 1982 and broken up at Aldenham by a contractor. Like most of the Routemasters up to RM 1210, RM 1206 was fulfilling the first role for this type – trolleybus replacement. There were fourteen replacement stages, running from 1959 to 1962 but delays in RM deliveries resulted in these vehicles only being used for stages 4-14. The last trolleybus depots were Fulwell and Isleworth, where electric operation ended on 8 May 1962. For this final stage, new bus routes and alterations to existing ones involved Fulwell (then becoming a bus garage), Norbiton and Hounslow. *(Bob Greenaway/Online Transport Archive)*

Continuing the unfortunate tradition in this book of portraying almost empty (or completely empty) Green Line coaches in Central London, RCL 2250 passes Trafalgar Square on its way from Godstone to Baker Street on 28 August 1974. The forty-three long Routemaster coaches of the RCL class were designed to provide a more luxurious alternative to the Liverpool Street steam-operated suburban 'Jazz' trains. However, they were no match for the newly electrified services and, following their introduction in May 1965 replacing RTs (which were only disguised standard buses), they started to be dispersed to other parts of the system from June 1966. By March 1972, all had been demoted to bus work apart from three (including RCL 2250), which were used on peak-hour workings on the 709 until March 1975 when un-luxurious Leyland National LNCs took over. RCL 2250 was purchased from LCBS by its former owners, LT, in March 1979 and given a convertible open top in 1991. The vehicle, now back in LT Green livery, currently serves as a mobile al fresco eating out experience in Bantham, Devon. *(Bob Greenaway/Online Transport Archive)*

Merlin MBA 606 hides behind a Routemaster as it passes the actual Marble Arch on its approach to Oxford Street on 28 August 1974. The bus is carrying a considerably less garish manifestation of the Chappell all-over advertising livery than that shown on page 50. Marble Arch was completed in 1833 and stood in the central courtyard of Buckingham Palace to form the state entrance. However, the Arch was dismantled in 1847 and moved to its present position to form a ceremonial entrance to the north east corner of Hyde Park. This was because Buckingham Palace was being enlarged, which involved building over the central courtyard to create a new east wing and form a uniform (flat) façade. Unfortunately, as mentioned on page 67, when Park Lane was widened in the early 1960s, Marble Arch became physically separated from Hyde Park and now stands on the present large traffic island. (*Bob Greenaway/Online Transport Archive*)

A red RT on route 146 (Bromley North station – Downe) sneaks into a picture depicting a trio of LCBS buses (two former RMC Green Line coaches painted in National Bus Company leaf green with, sandwiched between them, a Swift still in ex-LT Lincoln Green). The bus nearest the camera, RMC 1507 is bound for the 1974 Biggin Hill Air Display held in September. This vehicle entered Green Line service at Stevenage in January 1963 and passed to LCBS on 1 January 1970. The Company demoted the last of its RMCs from coach to bus work in April 1972 and sold RMC 1507 to LT in January 1978. The vehicle then became a trainer at Willesden until sold in September 1981. Happily, it is now preserved and restored to its original LT Green Line livery. *(Author's collection)*

LT suffered acute vehicle shortages several times during the 1970s, leading to various strange vehicles having to be hired from time to time. In 1975, LT was even reduced to using luxury coaches on two routes, the 125 and 270, borrowing them, with drivers, from Crouch End Coaches and Capital Coaches. The latter company also helped out on LT's Round London Sightseeing Tour, as evidenced in this shot of their Seddon Pennine 6 coach with Plaxton Panorama Elite body, new to Atkinson's of Chester-le-Street, Co Durham, in January 1972. The coach is seen here pulling out of Haymarket into Pall Mall on 26 April 1975, although one wonders if the tourists might have preferred to forfeit comfort for travel in a double decker. The name of this busy one-way street leading from Piccadilly to Pall Mall is, not surprisingly, derived from the fact that it was the location of a market for hay, straw and other agricultural products, situated in the countryside close to the village of Charing! The market moved in 1830, whereupon building development commenced. *(Bob Greenaway/Online Transport Archive)*

The yellow entrance doors help to break the monotony of the unrelieved all-red livery of DM 944 as it heads along Edgware Road on 13 July 1975. This crew-operated Fleetline entered service at Cricklewood in September 1974 and was withdrawn in October 1982, subsequently becoming a Playbus. Crew-operated DMSs had replaced RMs on route 16 (Victoria – Sudbury Town) on 15 December 1973 as a temporary measure pending the arrival of the purpose-built DMs (with no automatic fare collection machines), which superseded the DMSs on route 16 on 3 October 1974. Routemasters, in the form of RMLs, returned on 25 May 1980, replacing the DMs, so it was back to square one! The location of the photograph is at the Marble Arch end of Edgware Road and the splendid 1930's apartment block in the centre background stands on the corner of Harrowby Street. This building is the nine-storey Forset Court at 140 Edgware Road and forms part of the huge Portman Estate. *(Roger Harrison)*

One of the last scheduled daytime RT-operated routes into Central London was the 109 (Embankment – Purley), which was circular around the Thames in both directions and had replaced tram routes 16 and 18, which operated in the same way, on 8 April 1951. This view, dating from September 1975, depicts Thornton Heath's RT 1379 (since preserved) starting its southbound journey by crossing Westminster Bridge, having arrived at Embankment via Blackfriars Bridge. RTs were finally replaced on route 109 on 26 November 1976 and RT 1379, which had entered service with a Saunders roofbox body in July 1950 at Forest Gate, was withdrawn in February 1976 but escaped the scrapman. The tall brick building behind the bus is the Norman Shaw south building (Grade II listed), completed in 1906, and to its right is the original north building (Grade I listed), completed in 1890. These premises constituted New Scotland Yard until 1967 and are now ministerial offices. On the extreme right is another former Metropolitan Police edifice, the Curtis Green building, completed in 1940, which will shortly become the new Scotland Yard headquarters. Portcullis House (see page 59) has since replaced the buildings on the left. *(Martin Jenkins/Online Transport Archive)*

LCBS was experiencing particular vehicle shortages in 1975, mainly due to the unreliability of its Atlanteans (ANs), and set about borrowing buses. However, most unusually, the company actually bought three Northern Counties-bodied Leyland Titan PD3s from Southdown Motor Services after trialling some, basing them at Godstone garage, primarily for route 409. They were classified LS 1-3 (LS standing for Leyland Southdown) and entered service on 12 August 1975. Even more surprising was that LCBS did not bother to repaint them, so they remained in Southdown's attractive apple green and cream livery. The buses operated for almost a year, before being withdrawn in July 1976. This photograph, taken on 20 September 1975 at West Croydon bus station, shows LS 3 and also captures a DMS arriving on route 50 from Stockwell. LS 3 was new to Southdown in 1958 and vehicles of this type were nicknamed 'Queen Marys' because, with seating for sixty-nine passengers, they were so much larger than other crewed buses operating in Southdown's territory. Route 409 dated back to 1924 and operated from Croydon to Uckfield, until cut back to Forest Row on LT's creation in 1933 when a defined operating area for the new entity was set up. (C Carter/Online Transport Archive)

This conductor at Thornton Heath is finding out the hard way that setting the front blinds on a Leyland PD3/6 requires a balancing act that is not needed on normal London buses, which provide internal access to the mechanism. LT hired ten such Southend Corporation buses and put them to work from 22 September 1975 until the following February on route 190 (Thornton Heath – Old Coulsdon). These buses would clearly have been surplus to requirements outside the main seaside holiday season, which was why they became available. Their arrival at Thornton Heath garage enabled Routemasters to be released to fill gaps at other garages. When LT had finished with the vehicles they were borrowed by LCBS (see page 109) and sent to Harlow. The 190 was introduced on 8 April 1951 as a replacement for tram route 42 and had its southern terminus at South Croydon but this was extended to Old Coulsdon on 22 October 1952. RMs had superseded RTs on this service on 20 November 1971 and RMs returned after the hire of the PD3s had ended. *(C Carter/Online Transport Archive)*

Two unusual LCBS vehicles are seen at West Croydon bus station on 19 October 1975. In the foreground is SMA 4, an Alexander-bodied Swift belonging to a class of twenty-one originally ordered by South Wales Transport and diverted to LCBS. The whole class was allocated to the 725 south orbital Green Line service (Gravesend – Windsor, not via Central London) and entered service in 1972. Passengers appreciated the panoramic windows but the coaches were unreliable, exacerbated by the fact that they were underpowered, with mere 8.3 litre engines (by comparison, RFs had 9.6 litre engines). SMA 4 was withdrawn in December 1980. Behind this coach is MB4, a Strachans-bodied Merlin, which started its operational life in April 1966 as Red Arrow standee-type bus XMS 4, belonging to a batch classified XMS 1-6. A Country Area batch classified XMB 1-9 with increased seating was also produced. Now it gets complicated! XMB 2-9 were transferred to the Central Area, partially de-seated and renumbered XMS 7-14, leaving XMB 1 (now renumbered XMB 15 to maintain the Merlin number sequence) in green, this bus being transferred to LCBS in 1970. Meanwhile, XMS 4's interior was reconfigured with increased seating and it became MB 4. In November 1973, LT swapped it for XMB 15 (old XMB 1), whereupon MB 4 gained green livery and worked from Reigate garage. The bus was withdrawn at Windsor in February 1979, being sold for scrap, and in fact none of the fifteen distinctive Strachan-bodied Merlins survived to be preserved. *(C Carter/Online Transport Archive)*

As LCBS's vehicle shortages continued the company had to source more buses to hire and usually these were older vehicles whose operators would otherwise be withdrawing them. A typical case in point was Maidstone Borough Council Transport's Massey-bodied Leyland PD2As, six of which were hired to LCBS in November 1975. These buses dated from 1961-3 and were surplus to requirements as a result of the progressive conversion of Maidstone's services to one person operation, which was completed a year later. The PD2A's were put to work on route 499, releasing RMCs for other services. Here we see Maidstone No 23 on 24 January 1976 in Dartford High Street wearing the fiesta blue livery, which replaced the earlier ochre and cream that older readers will remember the trolleybuses carrying. One Maidstone PD2A, identical to the one pictured here, has been preserved, No 26 (26 YKO). *(Charles Firminger)*

As described on pages 96 and 99, LT was not without its troubles either and was reduced to buying second-hand buses in addition to hirings to alleviate vehicle shortages. As well as purchasing RTs (see page 106), LT also obtained the sixty-five BEA/BA Routemasters, which arrived in various tranches as the service between the West London Air Terminal and Heathrow began to decrease prior to cessation in 1979. Such was LT's desperation to use them that when the first thirteen arrived in August 1975, they received the minimum amount of attention (eg removal of luggage racks and trailer towing gear, but no repaint) before being sent to Romford (North Street) for use on route 175 (North Romford – Dagenham) from October 1975. This view in South Street, Romford, at the junction with Oldchurch Road, on 27 December 1975 illustrates the faded BEA orange livery on RMA 13 as it is passed by a demoted RCL Green Line coach. RMA 13 (ex-BEA 56) was sold for preservation in February 1987. The industrial building in the background has been converted into the Brickyard Bar and Grill. (Charles Firminger)

From December 1975 to June 1976, LCBS also hired six Eastbourne Borough Council AEC Regent Vs. These were 8-foot wide buses with East Lancs bodies. This view dating from 24 January 1976 shows Eastbourne No 68 in Market Street, Dartford, on route 477 passing the 1915-built Central Library and Bexleyheath's DMS 189 on a 96 service to Woolwich (a replacement for trolleybus route 696). The Regent V entered service at Eastbourne in May 1963, was withdrawn in June 1980 and is now preserved. The first buses to cover LCBS's vehicle shortages were some red RFs, initially loaned from the LT's Central Area to the Country Area, which became vehicle hires after the setting up of LCBS. These RFs were returned to LT between November 1970 and March 1971. More hired vehicles from LT arrived later in the form of some twenty red Merlins. LCBS already had their own RFs and Merlins so maintenance was not a problem, but when it came to hiring other buses, these were, as evidenced by these pictures, a mixed bunch and the owners were made responsible for the vehicles' maintenance. *(Charles Firminger)*

From November 1975 to March 1978, LCBS hired five Bournemouth Corporation 1965-built Weymann-bodied Daimler Fleetlines from a batch of ten on a rolling hire/maintenance basis. This surprisingly prolonged arrangement enabled the release of ANs at Leatherhead for other duties and here we see Bournemouth No 193 proceeding along Epsom High Street on 15 May 1976. Bournemouth Corporation ordered twenty such Daimler Fleetlines, the first ten (Nos 180-189) having removable fibreglass roofs and the remaining ten (Nos 190-199) having fixed roofs. Seven of the 'convertibles' were later bought by LT in 1977 (the DMO class, see page 162). Daimler Fleetlines were produced over a twenty year period starting in 1960, initially as a rival to the earlier Leyland Atlantean, and LT was the principal purchaser, amassing 2,646 vehicles (the DMS class) to supplement its eight XFs. The origins of Route 470 can be traced back to the pre-First World War 107/107A services, which were renumbered 70 in 1924 and 470 when LT took over. There was then a period through to 1939 when, unusually, the service was operated jointly by the Central Area and the Country Area. *(Neil Davenport)*

Kingston was one of many points where red and green buses met, and this view from June 1976 shows LCBS's RT 986 passing the ex-LGOC bus garage/bus station. This vehicle is showing signs of neglect, with a battered roof dome and a blind display which has gone awry, displaying route 406 (Kingston – Redhill) and route 406F (the race day service between Epsom station and Epsom Downs)! RT 986 entered service at Hertford in October 1948 and was withdrawn at Godstone in June 1977, followed by sale to a scrap merchant. Lurking in the shadows, surrounded by RFs, is RT 3185 which has an interesting history. Entering service at Amersham in June 1950, this bus remained in the Country Area and was transferred to LCBS in January 1970. It was then one of thirty-four such RTs re-acquired by LT in September 1972 (the first bulk purchase of second-hand vehicles by LT not involving the takeover of another operator) in order to help alleviate vehicle shortages. RT 3185 was withdrawn in August 1976 at Kingston and sold to a West German buyer. *(Author)*

In due course, the ex-BEA Routemasters used on route 175 (see page 103) did receive red livery and were also fitted with a canopy number box. However, the failure to fit destination indicators (there was just brief information on a slipboard), coupled with the absence of internal upright poles to grasp, made them unsuitable and unpopular for passenger work. Consequently, these buses were removed from the 175 in September 1976 and converted into trainers or staff buses running alongside later purchases of this type by LT. This photograph taken around July 1976 depicts RMA 4 (ex-BEA 29) at the Dagenham terminus, which was Ford Main Works. This bus ended its career as a trainer at Upton Park, where it was withdrawn in September 1990 and sold for scrap. *(Harry Luff/Online Transport Archive)*

Here is yet another hired bus, but this was not for overcoming LT's vehicle shortage. Following the popularity of the open top East Kent Guy Arabs in 1972 on the Round London Sightseeing Tour (see page 37), LT had contemplated removing the roofs from some RTs, but decided instead to enter into an initial three-year hire contract with Obsolete Fleet Ltd (owners of ST 922 used on vintage route 100) to provide open top buses to run alongside the DMs and DMSs on the Tour. The hired buses were seven specially converted (de-roofed) Midland Red D9s classified OM 1-7 and were based at Stockwell garage, entering service on 26 April 1975. OM 4, delivered to Midland Red in February 1963 (fleet number 5043) and withdrawn in May 1978, is standing in Grosvenor Gardens, within sight of Victoria station, around July 1976 but would now be facing the wrong way in a busy one-way street! This area is part of the Grosvenor Estate headed by the Duke of Westminster (who belongs to the Grosvenor family). In 1677, Sir Thomas Grosvenor acquired some 300 acres of farmland and marshland in Mayfair and Belgravia and went on to develop this ground into one of the wealthiest areas of the country. (*Harry Luff/Online Transport Archive*)

Another service to visit the Ford Motor Company, but this time at Brentwood rather than Dagenham, was route 339. Three buses wait outside Epping Underground station around September 1976, the front bus being demoted Green Line coach RMC 1483. Entering service at Epping in October 1962, shortly before this garage closed (on 21 May 1963) and replaced by Harlow garage, RMC 1483 passed to LCBS in 1970 and was re-acquired by LT in February 1980. After service as a trainer the bus was scrapped by LT in August 1989. Behind the Routemaster, stand two hired Southend Corporation Leyland PD3/6s with Massey bodies. These were the same vehicles that LT had borrowed (see page 100) and when that arrangement ceased the buses went to LCBS who based them at Harlow for route 339, replacing the last RTs stationed there, until they were returned to Southend in January 1977. The PD3/6 nearest the camera is CJN 434C, which was delivered to Southend Corporation in April 1965. Routemasters and RTs still operate services from Epping station using the 339 route number in connection with the Epping Ongar heritage railway. *(Online Transport Archive)*

To celebrate the Silver Jubilee of HM The Queen in 1977, twenty-five RMs were painted silver in February and carried advertising for various companies. These vehicles were allocated SRM numbers and entered service on 11 April, all but one being allocated to two or three different routes until 5 November, after which date they were repainted red. On Easter Sunday, 10 April 1977, all twenty-five, together with a refurbished RT (1599), a repainted RML (2661), a new DMS (2220) and a D9 open-topper (OM 4), took part in a cavalcade through Central London from Hyde Park to Battersea Park. This view at Trafalgar Square features RML 2661, DMS 2220, SRM 17 (RM 1894), SRM 7 (RM 1871) and, behind the statue of Sir Henry Havelock, SRM 22 (RM 1900). RML 2661 was sold to a Polish buyer in August 2003, DMS 2220 was withdrawn in November 1982 after less than six years LT service and scrapped in August 2000 following several changes of ownership and, of the three SRMs depicted, only SRM 7 survives today. (*Bob Greenaway/Online Transport Archive*)

SRM 3 (RM 1650) is overtaken by the first of two prototype Leyland Titans evaluated by LT prior to the placement of an order for 1,125 of these vehicles. This is prototype 004 of the type initially classified by Leyland as B15. It is operating on route 3 (Camden Town – Crystal Palace) and the picture is again taken at Trafalgar Square on 10 April 1977. SRM 3, an identity which it still carries today, has an interesting history. Entering service as RM 1650 at Cricklewood in July 1963, this bus was withdrawn at Bow in February 1985 and sold to Blackpool Transport. In 1997, it was acquired by Reading Mainline and later returned to London, re-entering service in December 2001 after refurbishment. In 2002, it lost its red livery in favour of gold vinyls to celebrate HM The Queen's Golden Jubilee. Now back in silver livery, this Routemaster joined Tower Transit's fleet in June 2013. *(Bob Greenaway/Online Transport Archive)*

Seemingly heading for The Mall and Buckingham Palace, but actually about to enter Whitehall on 10 April 1977 on its way to Battersea Park, SRM 1 (RM 1898) displays its Abbey National credentials as it leaves Trafalgar Square. The bus in the background to the right should need no introduction, being ST 922 working Vintage route 100 five years after it entered service following its remarkable renaissance. Sadly, RM 1898 did not enjoy a prolonged life as it was withdrawn in August 1985 and sold for scrap. Entry to The Mall from Trafalgar Square is through Admiralty Arch, which takes its name from the adjacent Old Admiralty Building, an edifice well known to the author who worked there in the (now defunct) Civil Service Department from 1977 to 1981. Admiralty Arch was commissioned by King Edward VII in memory of his mother, Queen Victoria, and was designed by Sir Aston Webb. Completed in 1912 after the King's death, the arch was disposed of by the Government in 2012 on a 125-year lease to a property developer who intends to convert it into a luxury hotel. (Bob Greenaway/Online Transport Archive)

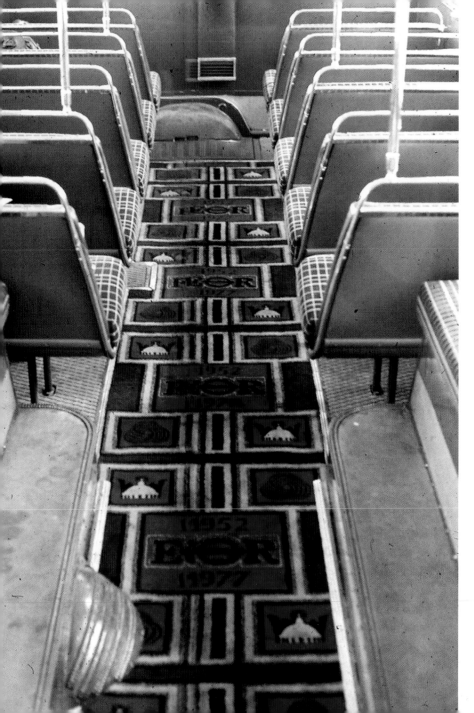

If readers find it hard to believe that London buses were ever carpeted, here is the proof! This is a view of the lower deck of SRM 6 (RM 1912) showing the Silver Jubilee carpet and also the extent to which the vehicle's drive shaft is not central, hence the hump in the floor by the nearside longitudinal seat (the differential cover) and the offset fly wheel cover at the front (a feature of RTs as well, which the author, as a child, believed to be a wholly inadequate heater for warming his cold hands!). During the six months or so that the SRMs worked normal services, special commemorative tickets were issued to passengers which carried on one side an advertisement for the bus sponsor which, in the case of SRM 6, was Townsend-Thoresen, the ferry company. Following its return to red livery in November 1977, RM 1912 continued in service until withdrawn at Camberwell in August 1985, whereupon it was exported to France, serving as a mobile catering establishment. *(Bob Greenaway/Online Transport Archive)*

There was great excitement among the enthusiast fraternity when continuing vehicle shortages caused LCBS to recertify four RTs, painting the three based at Chelsham into the NBC corporate livery of leaf green. The buses looked pristine although the overall effect was somewhat marred by ill fitting blinds. The first of the quartet to emerge was RT 1018 (now preserved) in April 1977 and it is seen in Chelsham's rear yard on 24 April. However, after some five months of passenger service RT 1018 was surplus and became a trainer at various garages until withdrawal in March 1981. The bus at the yard entrance with a dented and spotted roof dome (old Lincoln green livery showing through) is former Green Line coach RMC 1473. This vehicle was re-acquired by LT in January 1978 and used as a trainer until it was sold for scrap in August 1990. Chelsham garage opened on 20 January 1925 under the auspices of the East Surrey Traction Company and was closed on 29 June 1990, its existence being marked by a plaque on the wall of the supermarket now standing on the site. *(C Carter/Online Transport Archive)*

Route 403 (Wallington – Warlingham Park Hospital) was Chelsham's premier route and produced plenty of variety in bus types during the 1970s. From 5 March to 21 October 1977, up to nine Leyland Atlanteans hired from Maidstone Borough Council could be found on this busy and frequent service. This photograph, taken in June 1977 at Wallington, depicts Maidstone No 29, a Massey-bodied Atlantean dating from 1965. Route 403 started life on 16 August 1921 as East Surrey S3 (Sevenoaks – West Croydon), taking the number 403 on 1 December 1924 following the enactment of the London Traffic Act of 1924, which resulted in country services south of London entering the Metropolitan Police Area being numbered in the 400 series. East Surrey, operating in the south, was combined with the National Omnibus and Transport Co Ltd in the north to become London General Country Services in 1932, being subsumed into the London Passenger Transport Board (LT) in the following year. The Atlanteans, together with RTs and RMCs, were the mainstay of route 403 over the summer of 1977 until vehicle shortages eased. *(Harry Luff/Online Transport Archive)*

In this extraordinary picture of a deserted Regent Street, MD 134 overtakes SRM 11 (RM 1910) as both buses head for Piccadilly Circus on Sunday, 7 June 1977. The absence of people and traffic resulted from a Thanksgiving Service for HM The Queen taking place at St Paul's Cathedral, which involved royal carriage processions witnessed by around one million people, none of whom were in Regent Street! Also, there was no Sunday trading in this era. MD 134 belonged to the 164-strong class of Metro-Scania Metropolitans with MCW bodywork, which LT hoped would prove to be more successful than the unreliable Daimler Fleetlines and Leyland Atlanteans. However, the MDs were not an improvement and lasted barely seven years, mainly due to corrosion problems, shortage of spare parts and the arrival of better vehicles (Titans and Metrobuses). MD 134 entered service at New Cross around December 1976 and was withdrawn in September 1982, followed by scrapping. This was also the fate of RM 1910, which was withdrawn in November 1984. (*Bob Greenaway/Online Transport Archive*)

There is not much happening at Oxford Circus either on 7 June 1977, save for newly overhauled RM 747, devoid of advertisements, going about its business on route 12. The bus, based at Elmers End, is just pulling out of Oxford Street to turn into Regent Street, heading for Piccadilly Circus. Unfortunately, like so many standard Routemasters, it ended up in a scrapyard following withdrawal at Clapham in October 1986. The 12 is regarded by some as London's oldest bus route because the Oxford Circus – Peckham section was started in 1849 by Thomas Tilling with horse buses, these being superseded by motor buses on this route in 1904. The number 12 was first used by the LGOC from 10 December 1908 for a service between Turnham Green and Ilford Broadway via Oxford Street, which was altered to run between Turnham Green and Peckham when the LGOC and Tilling combined to operate the 12 from 8 May 1911. *(Bob Greenaway/Online Transport Archive)*

Kingston garage in Richmond Road was opened by the LGOC on 4 January 1922. This photograph depicts three of its residents in July 1977. RF 495 on the right is preserved and was noted for the strange colouring of its LT bullseye radiator cap cover plate. RT 4286 on the left entered service at Sutton in June 1953 and was withdrawn at Kingston in June 1979 following use as a trainer there, ending up with a scrap merchant. The same fate befell the middle vehicle, RT 1049, which entered service as a green bus at Leatherhead in December 1948. Both RTs had been recertified in late 1975/early 1976 for use on route 71 which was not converted from RT to RM operation (Mon-Sat) until 4 March 1978 (OPO single deckers were already in use on Sundays). This service had been introduced on 11 January 1950 to serve the Tudor Estate and the Ham Estate but was not the first route with this number to serve Kingston. Just prior to the First World War, this number was allocated to a service between Ealing Broadway and Surbiton, which subsequently became the 105 (not the Shepherds Bush/Heathrow one) and was later renumbered 65, which still runs today. *(Mike Harries/Author's Collection)*

Route 71 ran to Leatherhead garage from 30 November 1968 when it replaced the 65 and 65A beyond Surbiton until it was cut back to Surbiton from 31 March 1979, when the 265 (and now the 465) took over the southern end of the service. This August 1977 view shows RT 1139 on a 71 service standing at the entrance to the garage after turning round in the forecourt. Former modernised Green Line coach RF 79 also awaits its next bus duty. This vehicle was converted into a breakdown tender at Leatherhead following its first withdrawal in October 1977 and was sold after its second withdrawal in May 1982, later becoming a store shed. RT 1139 was sold for scrap following its withdrawal in June 1978. Subsequent to a co-operation agreement between the LGOC and East Surrey, Leatherhead garage was built in 1925, the entrance doors of which opened onto Guildford Road, beside the trees seen in this picture. The local council was concerned about the increase in bus movements when the garage was enlarged in 1939, so doors were fitted to the side of the garage, with vehicle access confined to the entrance shown here. Leatherhead garage closed on 30 April 1999. *(Mike Harries/Author's collection)*

One wonders whether the designers of the RT bus way back in 1937 could ever have imagined a sight like this forty years later – four RTs out on the road together still at work! This is Clarendon Road, Hayes, Middlesex (the stand for buses terminating at Hayes station) in August 1977, a time when RTs still operated routes 274 and 140, although the 274 (Ealing Broadway to Hayes) would lose its RTs soon after, with DMSs taking over on 1 October 1977. The RTs in question are 1599, 1301, 1641 and 4403. RT 1599, on the left, was the last of the class to be overhauled and repainted for further public service. This occurred in March 1977 so that it looked pristine for its role of leading the Silver Jubilee bus parade on 10 April. Withdrawn in March 1979, the bus has been preserved. RT 1301 (front right) was withdrawn at Barking in April 1979 and exported to the USA. RT 1641 (immediately behind RT 1301) was withdrawn in July 1978 and sold to a London buyer. Finally, RT 4403 (at the back) went for scrap following withdrawal in April 1978. *(Author)*

Growing up in North Ealing (apart from ten months in Edinburgh), the author developed an attachment to RTs, which operated his local 97 service out of Southall garage. He was therefore dismayed when, with much fanfare, leaflets were produced heralding the new E routes (E1, E2 and E3) with brand new driver-only buses, but was then delighted to find this modernisation counteracted by the introduction of two new RT-operated routes serving Ealing (the 273 and 274) on the same date (30 November 1968). The 273 (Ealing Broadway to Hayes) was converted to OPO on 6 January 1973 but the 274 (also Ealing Broadway to Hayes but with a different routeing) remained RT-operated until it was converted on 1 October 1977. This view, revealing arguably some of the worst examples of local architecture, depicts RT 4718 in Ealing Broadway in September 1977. The bus was withdrawn in October 1977 (i.e. on the 274's conversion) and was then sold for scrap. (Author)

This is Chiswick High Road in the morning rush hour around September 1977 and depicts a strange bus, 7517 UA, working from Richmond to Camden Town on route 27. This vehicle was originally Leeds City Transport No 717, a Roe-bodied Daimler CVG6 dating from 1959 which was purchased by Dennis and modified mechanically to test components that would be used in the proposed Dennis Dominator bus. In particular, the intention was to gauge the effectiveness of a Gardner 6LXB engine working with a Voith gearbox, a combination which produced a powerful vehicle. Dennis demonstrated 7517 UA to various operators including South Yorkshire PTE and Tayside Regional Council in the hope of encouraging interest in its new design which was Dennis's first rear-engine bus, marking the Company's return to bus building after a gap of several years. 7517 UA, which ended up being bought by Leicester Corporation for spares, spent its short time with LT, following its arrival in July 1977, based at Turnham Green and confined to route 27, working alongside Routemasters. *(Author)*

This is a final look at a Silver Jubilee-liveried Routemaster photographed at Oxford Circus a few days before the twenty-five vehicles in question were withdrawn on 5 November 1977 and repainted red. The subject of this picture, SRM 20 (RM 1899), advertising Avia Watches, entered service in May 1964 at Upton Park and was withdrawn at Elmers End in August 1985, before being scrapped. As an SRM, this vehicle had worked on routes 7 and 38 before its final allocation to Streatham for route 159. This service had a claim to fame for being the last to operate Routemasters on a full length route, this landmark event taking place on 9 December 2005. However, to stave off criticism that he had killed off a famous London icon, the Mayor of London introduced two heritage routes, 'touristy' sections of routes 9 and 15, to ensure that a handful of Routemasters remained on London streets, working alongside low floor buses operating the entire routes. Only route 15 now remains with 'old Routemasters' but crew operation on normal routes has returned, courtesy of the 'new Routemaster' (nicknamed 'Borismaster'!). (*Bob Greenaway/Online Transport Archive*)

Five LCBS RTs wore NBC leaf green livery: two trainers (RTs 2230 and 2367) and three of the four recertified in 1977, two of which are seen here on the forecourt of Chelsham garage around December 1977. These are RTs 604 and 3461, both of which have since been preserved along with the third (RT 1018) pictured on page 114. The recertified RTs emerged between April and June 1977 but were moved to training duties fairly quickly as newer buses became available. RTs 1018 and 3461 were transferred in September 1977, RT 981 in February 1978 (this was the fourth of the recertified quartet and remained in Lincoln green livery – it also survives today) and finally RT 604 which suffered engine failure in the summer of 1978, squashing any hopes of it outliving its red contemporaries once the only available spare engine was acquired for trainer RT 1018. Engineless RT 604 was eventually sold in July 1979 and, after receiving a replacement engine, remains very active today in its NBC leaf green livery. (*Martin Jenkins/Online Transport Archive*)

Route 146 (Bromley North station – Downe), which still operates today, has had a strange history, fluctuating with route 146A and sometimes being a Sundays only summer service, originally starting from Lewisham. The route as we know it today operated daily from 14 May 1952 using RTs, and this type continued to be used on the service until replaced by OPO BL single deckers on 22 April 1978. This was a bad day for RTs because, in addition to the 146, they were ousted from three other routes: the 54, 89 and 122, leaving just six RT daytime routes remaining. To find crew-operated RTs working such a rural service as late as 1978 surprised many people and this view of Bob Marley-adorned RT 785 captures the essence of the route as the bus heads towards Downe after descending New Road Hill. RT 785 entered service at Mortlake in August 1948 and was withdrawn at Bromley in May 1978, going for scrap. *(Dave Brown/Author's collection)*

London's most modern buses (not!) stand at Heathrow in April 1978 to greet travellers arriving at the world's busiest international airport – yes, they were old but at least they were reliable! Route 105, operated jointly by Southall and Shepherds Bush garages, lost its RTs on 30 April 1978, followed by the Harrow Weald-operated 140 service on 15 July 1978. The 105 from Shepherds Bush had been extended from Southall to Heathrow Central on 6 January 1973 and this view depicts the recently roofed bus station. On the left is RT 4018 which entered service at Streatham in January 1951 and was withdrawn at Hendon in December 1978, prior to its appointment with the scrap merchant. The other bus, RT 2143 fared somewhat better and was exported to Japan in May 1988. It had been withdrawn in May 1984, owing its longevity to the fact that it became a Chiswick skid pan bus in July 1979. Indeed, it was one of only three RTs to remain in stock upon LT's demise on 29 June 1984, following the formation of London Regional Transport. (Author)

By 1978 an influx of new drivers and expiring MOTs in the training fleet resulted in a shortage of instruction vehicles. Consequently, the training fleet needed topping-up so LT took the unprecedented step of hiring preserved RTs and RTLs. This occurred for two periods in 1978, the first taking place in April. Four RTs were hired from 4 April, one of which was RT 191 seen here leaving Chiswick Works, followed a week later by a further six. All were returned on 1 May. RT 191 originally entered service at Leyton in October 1947 and was withdrawn in December 1962. The bus then passed through commercial hands twice before being purchased for preservation in October 1966. It carries an early RT3 type body (not its original one but an identical one which it received at overhaul in April 1957). The white relief around the lower deck windows is incorrect for a post-war RT but in its current active preserved state it now carries an authentic livery for its type. *(Author)*

From 28 April 1973 until 7 July 1978 the author had the pleasure of being able to watch RTs from his sofa! Having left the parental residence in Ealing on getting married, the first home of his own was a downstairs maisonette in High Street, Harlington, almost opposite West End Lane. The RTs in question were Harrow Weald-based and working route 140 from Mill Hill to Heathrow Airport, sharing the service on Sundays with Edgware-based Routemasters. RT 3234, seen here in Shaftesbury Avenue, South Harrow at the junction with Merton Road and Dudley Road in May/June 1978, was selected to work the final RT duty on 14 July 1978 and was festooned with balloons and streamers inside, with the Union flag fluttering from an upstairs front window and a wreath and ceremonial notice attached to the radiator. However, its glory was short lived as the bus was withdrawn in January 1979 at Wood Green where it had become a trainer before being sold for scrap. *(Author)*

The 140 was fully converted to RT operation from 14 May 1952, before which there had been a phased takeover from RTLs and RTWs, and the route was extended from Hayes to London Airport Central (now Heathrow) on 4 May 1955. Towards the end of the RT class's tenure, Harrow Weald was beginning to experience problems with blind displays as these two shots illustrate. The **above left** picture depicts RT 2882 in High Street, Harlington, at the junction with West End Lane (and about to pass the author's maisonette!). Whereas this bus went for scrap, the one in the **above right** picture struck lucky. The vehicle is RT 4772 and is seen in High Street, Harlington, approaching Harlington Corner and about to pass the Aerial Hotel on the right. This bus, originally green, was completed in June 1954 and entered service at Hemel Hempstead in June 1959 (it was stored for five years, being part of a batch which was surplus to requirements due to over-ordering). Withdrawn at Alperton in February 1979, RT 4772 was purchased by Abegweit Tours, Prince Edward Island, Canada and was repatriated in October 2010 along with ten other pristine, operational ex-Abegweit London buses (six more RTs, two RTLs and two RMs). (*Author – both*)

Sunday afternoons were interesting for route 140/RT followers because two journeys to Heathrow (and two return journeys) avoided Harlington and the A4 Bath Road. Instead, they ventured into Shepiston Lane to stop at Cherry Lane cemetery and then proceeded to Heathrow using the M4 airport spur, creating the unusual spectacle of RTs hammering down a motorway on a bus route. Latterly, special blinds on a yellow background were used to distinguish the four trips, as evidenced in this view taken of the final working of the day outside the cemetery gates in June 1978. Two passengers have alighted, presumably to visit a grave, while the third person is a photographer desperate not to miss the bus, otherwise he would have to wait a week for the next one to come! The RT is 3220, which entered service as a green bus at Staines in July 1950 and became a mobile disco in Spain when exported in September 1982. *(Author)*

Like RT 191 on page 127, this is another preserved bus on hire to LT which is wearing an incorrect livery for its type. RT 1320, seen leaving Chiswick Works on driver training duties in June 1978, is one of the 300 RTs (see also page 16) with bodies constructed by the Saunders Engineering Shipyard Ltd (later renamed Saunders-Roe (Anglesey) Ltd). The Saunders RTs were all Central Area red buses throughout their lives, so none were green. However, externally the Saunders RTs, with their front roofboxes, closely resembled the early post-war RTs, the main distinguishing feature being the positioning of the offside route stencil plate. Therefore, RT 1320's colour scheme, which is early post-war country livery, is authentic, but incorrect for a Saunders RT. This bus entered service at Willesden in February 1950 and was sold to the London Borough of Waltham Forest in July 1969 before being purchased for preservation in September 1976. In this photograph, RT 1320 has recently arrived for its second stint as a hired trainer which started on 26 June 1978 and lasted until 1 November. *(Author)*

The second tranche of training vehicle hirings involved nine RTs and five RTLs which were returned to their owners at various times up to 1 November 1978. The arrival of RTLs was particularly noteworthy since the last examples of these Leyland Titans had been withdrawn from public service on 29 November 1968 and from non-public duties on 1 October 1970. This shot depicts a very dated-looking RTL 326 as it is about to turn into Chiswick Works in August 1978. This bus had entered service at Tottenham in August 1949 and therefore would have worn the livery shown here when new, as the all-red livery with cream central waist band was not introduced on newly delivered RTLs until April 1950. It would also have entered service with a restricted blind display as depicted here – a wartime measure resulting from a shortage of linen and the need to minimise lighting during the blackout. RTL 326 was withdrawn at Stonebridge Park in July 1966 and then passed through several hands both before and during its current life in preservation. *(Author)*

This could be your author at the wheel of RF 506 as he worked for Continental Pioneer of Richmond on a part-time basis between the late 1960s and early 1980s driving (mainly) the Company's RTLs and RFs and Ted Brakell's RMFs, the Brakell vehicles sharing the former Richmond goods yard site with Pioneer and various preservationists. This picture is taken in Church Road, Richmond Hill, at the junction with Kings Road in July 1978, on route 235. LT operated this service linking Richmond station and Richmond Hill (a six-minute journey) until 29 January 1966 when it was suspended, along with several other routes, as a result of an overtime ban. These services were offered to independent operators temporarily but when the industrial dispute ended and LT resumed services, the 235 was one of two not reinstated. Isleworth Coaches became the operator from 21 February 1966 and Pioneer took over in May 1968. They gave up the service on 27 September 1980 and LT's route 71 was diverted to serve Richmond Hill instead. *(C Carter/Online Transport Archive)*

This bus is living up to its description of offering a 'multi-ride' because it appears to be full to overflowing, with restricted vision for the driver! The lowbridge double deckers were replaced on the 248 (see pages 22 and 23) on 19 September 1970 by OPO Swifts and the route revised, which included a western extension to Hornchurch and Romford. The Swifts on this service were superseded by Leyland Nationals from 26 February 1978 and this view was taken soon after, depicting LS 120 pulling away in Hornchurch Road, Romford. LT purchased 506 Leyland Nationals between 1973 and 1981 to replace the unsuccessful Swifts and Fleetlines and this example entered service at Romford for use on the 248 in February 1978 following the removal of the Swifts. The bus ended its LT life working from Bexleyheath in January 1991 and was sold, eventually being withdrawn and cannibalised in 2000. (*John May/Online Transport Archive*)

Still in Lincoln green livery in September 1978 but looking somewhat neglected, London Country RML 2314 threads its way through South End, Croydon on its way from West Croydon bus station to Reigate. This vehicle spent its entire Country bus career at Godstone garage, from its entry into service in October 1965 to its withdrawal in early 1979. Purchased by LT in July 1979, RML 2314 embarked on its second career, becoming a red bus, and was withdrawn from New Cross garage in January 2005 before being exported to Canada the following year. In this view it is being pursued by a DMS vehicle working local Croydon service C1. (*Author*)

The first LT Metro-Cammell-Weymann (MCW) Metrobus, MT I, stands on display at the National Showbus Rally, Hillingdon, on 24 June 1978. The National Showbus Rally began as a small display of buses held in the staff car park of Brunel University, Uxbridge, in 1973, but due to the 1974 date having to be deferred because of the disruption to economic life caused by the miners' strike, the rally was combined with the annual Hillingdon Show, until a larger venue was required in 1980. Several new generation buses were exhibited at Hillingdon in 1978 but a Leyland Titan, which was due to be exhibited, failed to attend. A few days after this picture was taken, MT 1 was renumbered M1, possibly to avoid adverse references to 'empty one'! MT 2 and MT 3 were also renumbered, whereas subsequent vehicles never carried the T designation. (*Bob Greenaway/Online Transport Archive*)

Route 94 from Bromley to Lewisham was the third last RT-operated LT service and was fully converted to RM operation on 26 August 1978. This route had a claim to fame insofar as it was worked by RTs for the longest period of any route, from 3 May 1950 for Bromley and 11 October 1950 for Catford, both garages being involved for the entire period of operation. Against a most unattractive backdrop near Petts Wood station on the last day of RT-operation, RT 449 sets off for Bromley garage. On arrival, Driver Wade, an RT enthusiast, stands in front of his much-loved bus, with his conductor. Sadly, RT 449 was shortly to take the well-trodden path to the famous (or perhaps infamous!) Wombwell scrapyard in South Yorkshire. *(Author)*

The flowers are blooming at Southgate Circus in summer 1978 as SMS 371 heads for the bus station behind the iconic, circular Underground station in order to terminate there. The bus was new to Merton in January 1971 and was withdrawn at Potters Bar in July 1980, before heading for the scrapyard. Route 299 (Southgate – Borehamwood) was a new service introduced on 24 January 1970 to replace part of the 298 and was worked from Potters Bar garage, initially with RTs. The service was converted to OPO using Swifts on 3 July 1971 and these remained, supplemented at times by DMS double deckers, until the route was withdrawn on 27 September 1980 when it was superseded by the route it replaced, the 298, albeit a revised version. (John May/Online Transport Archive)

Following trials with a Demonstrator, LT ordered twenty Ford Transits with manual gearboxes and Strachans sixteen-seater bodywork (classified FS) on four new minibus routes which it had identified. FS 19 entered service in August 1973 at Stockwell for the P4 route and was later transferred to Finchley for the new Dial-a-Ride circular service. Introduced on 19 October 1974, this ran between Golders Green and Hampstead Garden Suburb and later became the H2 route which still runs today, but not using tiny FSs! FS 19 was converted into a radio trainer associated with the Busco (Bus control and communications system) trials on Peckham's RMs operating on the 36 group of routes which were particularly susceptible to irregular running due to traffic congestion. FS19 lasted from May 1983 to March 1986 in this role before being sold in September 1986 and later scrapped. This photograph was taken at Golders Green station in summer 1978. *(John May/Online Transport Archive)*

Holloway's Route C11 (Archway – Cricklewood Broadway) started on 28 October 1972 using FS minibuses (see page 139) but when the service was extended from Cricklewood to Willesden Green on 16 October 1976 the Ford Transit/Strachans were replaced by more substantial small buses, the BS class. These were short wheel base Bristol LHS vehicles, just 24 foot long, with Eastern Coachworks twenty-six-seat bodywork, and with unwelcome manual gearboxes, in fact some might say just a more modern looking, but uglier, Guy Special (GS)! This view dates from summer 1978 and depicts BS 6 having passed the Archway Tavern at 7 Archway Road. The reign of the BSs on the C11 was not very prolonged because on 30 March 1981 larger BLs took over and BS 6 found itself up for sale. *(John May/Online Transport Archive)*

Romford North Street's RM 1712 meets Barking's RT 778 in Dagnam Park Drive, Harold Hill in late August 1978. The purpose of visiting this location was to photograph the RTs on route 87 before their imminent demise and, while the author was setting up the shot, the Routemaster swept by unannounced. This bus was working route 174 (Dagenham – Romford) which was introduced on 3 May 1950 as a replacement for the 86B. The service was extended a few months later to Harold Hill and in 1958 reached Noak Hill. Partial conversion from RTs to RMs occurred from 10 July 1966 and full conversion from 20 April 1974. RM 1712 entered service at Holloway in October 1963 and was withdrawn at Merton in June 1984, from where it went for scrap. The same fate befell RT 778 after withdrawal at Riverside in March 1979 following a short spell as a trainer. *(Author)*

Opportunities to photograph RTs together working the last two routes, the 87 and 62, were limited but the photographer has succeeded in East Street, Barking, on a section of road which is now pedestrianised. The date is 9 September 1978 and the buses are outside the old Barking Magistrates Court at 44-48 East Street which was completed in 1893 and closed in 2011. The Flemish-Renaissance style building is Grade II listed and is due to be converted into a restaurant and residential apartments. The buses featured are, from left to right, RT 379 and RT 3254, the latter being the luckier of the two, for it entered service in Green Line livery in August 1950 at Romford and has been restored to this livery today, following preservation. RT 379, on the other hand, having been transferred from Barking to Alperton as a trainer following conversion of the 87 to Routemasters (apart from one Saturday duty) on 28 October 1978, was withdrawn in July 1979 and sold for scrap. *(Alan Murray Rust/Online Transport Archive)*

RTs still rule in Longbridge Road, Barking, on 21 October 1978 in this view close to Barking garage (just visible behind the retreating 87 bus). The two identifiable vehicles are RT 3321 in the foreground and RT 3016 behind, both of which enjoyed afterlives. The former entered service at Catford in October 1951 and moved to Barking in April 1978. Following the replacement of RTs by RMs on route 87 from 28 October 1978, one week after this picture was taken, RT 3321 was sold to a West German buyer. RT 3016 started its operational career at Middle Row (North Kensington) in May 1953 and was withdrawn following the last day of RT operation on route 62 on 7 April 1979, after which it travelled to France as an exhibition unit. Barking garage was opened by the LGOC in 1924 and is currently used by Stagecoach. (*Roger Harrison*)

While visiting Staines bus garage (the building on the right) on 28 January 1979, the cameraman has taken the opportunity to photograph BL 8 on its way to the terminus at the former Staines West railway station. LT bought ninety-five Bristol BLs, primarily as replacements for the aging RFs, particularly for services where Leyland Nationals were unsuitable, for example at Kingston where the inspection pits were small. However, contractions in services on which they were used, coupled with unreliability problems and shortage of spares (a familiar story), meant that some had an extraordinarily short life, such as BL 8 which entered service in September 1976. This bus was withdrawn in March 1980, despite being repainted in October 1979, sold in March 1982, and subsequently scrapped. The other two buses visible in this view are a Leyland National on route 116 to Hammersmith which has just reached the confusing Crooked Billet junction and an RF working a 218 service passing the bus garage. (Charles Firminger)

On 30 March 1979, the operating agreement between LT and British Airways (which subsumed the former BEA) was terminated due to the withdrawal of the service between the West London Air Terminal and Heathrow from that date. The service had been reduced over several years, resulting in batches of Airport Routemasters being acquired by LT in 1975, 1976 and 1978. At the end, only twenty-nine of these Routemasters remained with British Airways, including NMY 662E, seen here in early 1979 with its trailer and a few airline passengers aboard, outside the Air Terminal in Cromwell Road, a site now occupied by a well known supermarket retailer. LT designated the vehicle RMA 62 when they acquired it in June 1979, using it initially as a staff bus between Leyton and Aldenham. After being made redundant by LT's successors, the vehicle has been put to a variety of uses: playbus, mobile caravan, part of a 'peace convoy' to Baghdad and election bus for the Green Party! (*Bob Greenaway/Online Transport Archive*)

The photographer certainly moved around on 24 March 1979 because, not only was he at Kingston on that day (see following photographs) but also in Exhibition Road, South Kensington, where he spotted 'Basil Bus' ex-RT 4782 passing the Victoria & Albert Museum (the corner of which is just visible on the left), with Cromwell Road behind. RT 4782 was delivered in July 1954 and was one of those stored for five years as a result of LT over-ordering, entering service at Dunton Green in June 1959. At overhaul at Aldenham in December 1968, the bus changed from green to red livery and was sent to New Cross where it remained until premature withdrawal in October 1973. It was then sold and at the time of this photograph was owned by Fads Homecare. In January 1989, its body was scrapped and the chassis used for a glider winch. (*Bob Greenaway/Online Transport Archive*)

LCBS appear to have abandoned this Leatherhead-based Leyland National at the bus stand alongside Kingston station on 24 March 1979 because, not only is it completely empty, but the front blind states 'Private'. Maybe it has broken down although, to be fair, despite these vehicles being noisy and rattling, they were generally reliable. The vehicle is SNB (Short National Bus) 392, one of 168 of the cheap, basic Series B Leyland Nationals purchased by the Company to replace their unreliable Merlins and Swifts and distinguishable externally from other versions by the absence of the air-conditioning pod on the roof. SNB 392 entered service at Leatherhead in November 1978 and, after transfer to LCBS successor companies, was withdrawn in 1997 and sold for further service. (Bob Greenaway/Online Transport Archive)

On 24 March 1979 the photographer has managed to capture two learner buses together as they pass Kingston railway station. In front is ex-Green Line coach RCL 2247, purchased by LT following its withdrawal at Grays in October 1978. The London Country fleet name and NBC emblem have been painted over and a white LT roundel applied. In 1980, at considerable expense, LT converted the coach into a bus, removing doors, luggage racks, ash trays and twin headlights, and installing vertical interior poles. It then joined other converted RCLs on route 149 (Ponders End – Victoria) starting on 27 September 1980, replacing crewed Fleetlines (DMs). Whether the conversion costs were worthwhile is however debatable because the RCLs were replaced by normal Routemasters from 16 December 1984, whereupon RCL 2247 was withdrawn and sold for scrap. Catford trainer RT 686, behind the RCL, also suffered the same fate when it was withdrawn in October 1979. (Bob Greenaway/Online Transport Archive)

On the last Saturday of LT scheduled RF operation, 24 March 1979, RF 502 travels along Portsmouth Road, Kingston to Staines on a 218 service. This route started life numbered 62 by the LGOC on 4 January 1922 from Kingston to Shepperton and was extended to Staines on 16 May 1923, taking the number 218 in October 1934. RFs replaced TDs on this route on 6 January 1960 and were themselves superseded by Leyland Nationals on 31 March 1979. The RFs at Kingston had been due for withdrawal in 1976 but there were insufficient Bristol BLs to replace them. Larger single deckers could not be used because they were too big to fit over the inspection pits at Kingston while double deckers were unsuitable for the 218 due to several low bridges. The problem was eventually resolved by transferring the route to Norbiton garage, but in the meantime twenty-five RFs were overhauled for continued operation including this one, RF 502, which unusually still carries a gold fleet number and name rather than a white number and large bullseye. Many of the 700-strong RF fleet have been preserved, but not RF 502 which went for scrap in December 1979. *(Bob Greenaway/Online Transport Archive)*

This is a sight which will please RF enthusiasts, particularly the current owner of RF 512 which is now preserved! It is still the final Saturday of RF scheduled operation in London, 24 March 1979, and BL 51 has broken down outside Kingston bus station/garage on a route 216 working. Passengers have been rescued by RF 512. The 216 (Kingston – Staines via Sunbury and Ashford) was officially converted to BL operation on 26 September 1976 although RFs occasionally substituted. This route started from the railway station forecourt rather than the bus station so the passengers appear to have travelled little more than a couple of hundred yards before the BL conked out! With some Country Area routes already converted to OPO, LT had intended to follow suit in the Central Area in 1959, with a selection of routes including the 216, but the previous agreement with the unions had expired in 1949 following the withdrawal of the red twenty-seater Leyland Cubs. Several RFs were converted for OPO, with doors added, but had to be crewed until union agreement was obtained in 1964, the 216 being converted from 18 November 1964. *(Bob Greenaway/Online Transport Archive)*

Route 219 (Kingston – Weybridge station) shared with the 218 the distinction of being the last RF-operated service, and this view dating from 24 March 1979 depicts the last Saturday working to the British Aerospace Works at Brooklands. The extension of certain journeys on the 219 from the railway station to what was then the Vickers Works (BAC from 1964) began in January 1938, and between 1942 and 1945 buses serving the Works and satellite buildings nearby, such as the former Cobham Bus Museum in Redhill Road, were painted grey including one of the London Bus Museum's unrestored vehicles, T357, which was based at Addlestone for route 462 and discovered in France in 2002. The bus seen here at Brooklands, RF 502, was sold for scrap in December 1979 but three RFs can presently be found on the reduced Brooklands site, in the London Bus Museum, these being RF 19 (sightseeing coach), RF 226 (Green Line coach) and RF 395 (Central Area bus). Here's a sobering thought: the little girl in the photograph will today be in her forties! (Author)

Now we have reached the last day of RF-operation, Friday 30 March 1979, and grubby RF 481 stands beside a shiny Leyland National, LS 53, in the forecourt of the former Staines (West) railway station (originally a rich man's villa, then a poor railway promoter's building and now converted into smart offices). On the following day, it would be two Leyland Nationals together. The 117 (Hounslow – Staines) was originally introduced in this area in 1916 but the route was re-organised to resemble its 1970s incarnation in 1922, although over the years its eastern and western extremities have been reduced. Routemasters were replaced by OPO LS vehicles from 28 January 1978. LS 53 entered service at Hounslow in September 1976 and was withdrawn at West Ham in February 1990. RF 481 entered service at Muswell Hill in February 1953 and was withdrawn following conversion of the 219 the day after this picture was taken and sold for scrap. *(Bob Greenaway/Online Transport Archive)*

Eight days after the end of the RFs, it was the turn of the RTs to be withdrawn from passenger service. The last RT route was the 62 which had been scheduled for conversion to Routemasters in October 1978, along with the 87, but staff would not agree to the conversion because of the extra width of the RMs and the narrowness of Chadwell Heath station bridge, coupled with the poor road surface there. The solution was to divert the route and a conversion date of the 31 March was proposed, but then put back to 7 April to avoid clashing with a commemorative RF tour at Kingston. Consequently, the RT class just managed to reach its fortieth year of passenger service. This photograph of the inside of Barking garage was taken on 31 March 1979 and the three identifiable buses went on to have very different futures. RM 523 was scrapped in 1985, RT 2240 next to it was rebuilt into a triple decker, with parts from RTs 3882 and 4497 for the Harry Potter film *The Prisoner of Azkaban*, and RT 4633, in the centre, left Barking for the Niagara Falls in Canada and later moved to Belgium. *(Bob Greenaway/Online Transport Archive)*

If Ensignbus have discovered any structural weaknesses in their preserved RT 624, this photograph might provide an explanation! With streamers hanging from some windows (they are not scratches on the original colour slide!), RT 624 struggles past the Bull Hotel at 2 North Street, Barking on 7 April 1979, working the last official RT service. The bus is not surprisingly full of enthusiasts witnessing the end of an era, so a duplicate bus, RM 208, preceded the RT to pick up 'normal passengers'. RT 624 arrived back at Barking garage at 1.45pm and then took its place in a ceremonial cavalcade involving six Barking buses and headed by the wonderfully restored RT1 which, only some six months earlier, had been a wreck rotting inside West Ham garage in the guise of mobile instruction unit 1037J. *(Bob Greenaway/Online Transport Archive)*

A twenty-six-seater horse bus dating from around 1875 and operated by Thomas Tilling for some twenty years, stands alongside a newly delivered MCW Metrobus, M 30, at Chiswick Works on 9 April 1979. Thomas Tilling started his London services in 1846 which were well patronised compared with rival operators because they stopped at predetermined points according to a timetable. Consequently, they were nicknamed the 'Times' buses and this was adopted as the slogan painted on the sides of his vehicles. The horse bus has so-called 'knifeboard' seating upstairs (a long central bench with passengers sitting back to back), a type which was abandoned in favour of the 'garden seat' configuration in common use today (i.e. pairs of seats facing forwards with a central gangway). M30 entered service in April 1979 at Fulwell and became a trainer in 1997, before being sold in 2002. As evidenced in this view, M30 has been delivered with white relief around the upper windows. Metrobuses from M56 onwards were painted in all-red livery. (Bob Greenaway/Online Transport Archive)

RM 2189 is well patronised on 14 April 1979 as it leaves Hyde Park Corner and enters Knightsbridge on the unsuccessful Shop Linker route. This service, operating out of Stockwell, was introduced on 7 April 1979, for which sixteen Routemasters were painted in this striking red and yellow livery and fitted with a public address system for the playing of music and the inevitable advertisements. The intention was to have all the buses sponsored (this one is advertising Burberry's/Scotch House) but some remained unsponsored. The route was circular, starting and finishing at Marble Arch and visiting Oxford Street, Regent Street and Knightsbridge, thus serving several West End major stores, and all for a flat fare of 30p. However, the operation was not sufficiently well supported by shoppers/tourists and ran for the last time on 28 September 1979. RM 2189 was withdrawn in July 1992 and sold for scrap. (Bob Greenaway/Online Transport Archive)

Photographed at Battersea Park's Easter Parade on 15 April 1979 was this Swift, SPB 753, formerly SMS 753. A long term resident of Harrow Weald from October 1971, one month after its entry into service, until withdrawal there in August 1978, this vehicle was converted into a mobile shop and information centre, primarily to support the various major events and celebrations taking place in 1979 such as the farewell RT cavalcade at Barking and the 150th Anniversary of the first London bus service. The anniversary was also marked by the Easter Parade bus rally where a cavalcade of buses filed through Battersea Park including the LT Museum's newly restored operational RT making its first public appearance, RT 4712, (as opposed to the Museum's static representative, RT 4825) and appropriately carrying route 62 blinds. SPB 753 was sold in 1985 and has since been preserved. *(Bob Greenaway/Online Transport Archive)*

On 3 September 1977, Hillingdon Council became the first London borough to operate its own bus service when new route 128 (Ruislip – Harefield/Rickmansworth) was inaugurated, using two Bristol BLs (joined by a third a year later). LT was the operating agent for Hillingdon, purchasing the vehicles, maintaining and garaging them (at Uxbridge), and driving them, with the Council picking up the costs. As shown in this picture of BL 94 at Ruislip in spring 1979, the buses wore a distinctive red and yellow livery with yellow blinds (perhaps this inspired the Shop Linker livery), although a larger amount of yellow was applied when the buses were repainted in 1981/2. Leyland Nationals replaced the BLs from 13 July 1988 but their use was short-lived as the service was withdrawn on 17 August 1991. BL94 entered service at Uxbridge in September 1977 specifically for this route, along with now preserved BL 95, and was withdrawn at Uxbridge in July 1988. The vehicle then passed through several owners' hands, including a ten year stint with Guernseybus, and was converted into a caravan in 2001. *(John May/Online Transport Archive)*

The highlight of the 150th anniversary celebrations in 1979 was surely the painting of several buses in an adaptation of Shillibeer's livery of 1829. George Shillibeer (1797-1866) was a Londoner who learned his trade as a coach builder in the Covent Garden area and obtained work in Paris where he was asked to build some extra-large coaches for a public omnibus service there. He then returned to London to do the same here, but this time for himself, building a single decker to carry some twenty passengers pulled by three horses abreast. This enabled him to start London's first public omnibus service on 4 July 1829, operating between Paddington and Bank. Shillibeer's pioneering service generated considerable competition which unfortunately he was unable to rival and within ten years he retired from coach operation and was largely forgotten. However, he was remembered in 1929, when a replica coach was constructed, and again in 1979, through the recreation of his ornate livery, as portrayed here by Watneys-sponsored RM 2191 entering Trafalgar Square from Strand on a mid-summer's evening. (Roger Harrison)

The driver of Shillibeer-liveried RM 2208 must be feeling the heat on 20 June 1979 because both sections of the windscreen have been opened. Twelve RMs and one Fleetline (DM 2646) received the Shillibeer treatment for operation on various routes up to 30 November 1979, together with mobile cinema and exhibition bus RCL 2221 and RM2, the guinea pig for this livery. RM 2208 was sponsored by North Thames Gas and worked from Walthamstow, West Ham and Leyton garages and was based at West Ham when seen here in Holborn, after passing Holborn Circus. The unfinished building on the left is Jeygrove Court, an apartment block on the corner of Holborn and Hatton Garden. Unlike RM 2191 on the previous page which was broken up in 1988, RM 2208 lives on. It was sold to Clydeside Scottish following withdrawal at Thornton Heath in February 1987 and entered preservation in May 1993. Remarkably, it looks the same today as it does in this picture. *(Neil Davenport)*

There do not appear to be many, if any, empty seats on this Metro-Scania, MD 135, as it pulls out of Whitehall into Trafalgar Square in summer 1979 on a short working of route 53 (Camden Town – Plumstead). The problems with this vehicle type are covered on page 116 but at least MD 135 was not scrapped at the end of its brief six-year service life with LT because, on its withdrawal at Plumstead in September 1982, it was sold to another operator. The origins of the present route 53 can be traced back to 1913 but, with changes in routeing and renumbering as 53A, it becomes rather complicated; but suffice it to say that the 53 number was reinstated in place of 53A in 1952. MDs replaced RMs on 8 January 1977, but on 31 October 1981, the RMs were back! These continued to operate the service until it was converted to OPO on 16 January 1988. *(Roger Harrison)*

Enthusiastic schoolchildren show their delight at being aboard the Stockwell Princess (DMO 1) in summer 1979. Bournemouth Corporation bought ten Weymann-bodied Daimler Fleetlines with detachable fibreglass roofs in 1965 to supplement their closed-top fleet (see page 105) and LT bought seven of these in October 1977 for the Round London Sightseeing Tour following the ending of the three year contract with Obsolete Fleet for the hire of the ex-Midland Red D9s. DMO 1 (ex-Bournemouth No 182 'Warwickshire') had spent a month at Leatherhead garage on hire to LCBS in August 1977 and entered service with LT at Stockwell in April 1978, along with the other six vehicles, following modifications at Aldenham which included the fitting of a public address system. The first three were initially named (DMO 1 was Stockwell Princess, DMO 2 was Southern Queen, DMO 3 was Britannia) but only DMO 1 retained its name. All were withdrawn in July 1981 except DMO 3 which lasted until October 1984. DMO 1 was sold to a Swedish operator for use on the island of Gotland. (John May/Online Transport Archive)

M1, the doyen of the M class of MCW Metrobuses numbering 1,440 vehicles, turns out of Park Lane to pass Marble Arch on its way from Victoria to Cricklewood in summer 1979. When delivered in April 1978. M1 was unique in having a black 'skirt' and retained this throughout its London operating life. It began life at Cricklewood in November 1978 working as a crewed bus alongside Routemasters on the 16 and 16A and ended when it was sold to Ensignbus for preservation in January 2008, having been used as a trainer since 1997. LT's preferred choice for replacement of the Merlins, Swifts and Fleetlines was the Leyland Titan but deliveries were never going to keep up with operating requirements so the Metrobus was chosen to supplement the Titans in the role of updating the LT bus fleet for the 1980s and 1990s, a sound decision given that some lasted on London routes into the new Millennium. *(John May/Online Transport Archive).*

It is time for a final look at the splendid Shillibeer livery as RM 2204 pulls up behind RM 1902 on Holborn Viaduct while working route 22 (Putney – Homerton) on 20 August 1979. RM 2204 entered service at Hackney in May 1965 and spent its Shillibeer period working from West Ham (route 25), Battersea (route 22, as seen here) and Palmers Green (route 29). The bus was withdrawn at Leyton in December 1991 and sold for scrap. Holborn Viaduct was opened by Queen Victoria in 1869 and was central London's first flyover. The main part of the Viaduct spans Farringdon Road/Farringdon Street but the section of railings visible in the picture is at the western end where it crosses Shoe Lane. Atlantic House, the buildings behind the buses, dates from 1951 and was occupied by Her Majesty's Stationery Office (HMSO) until 1984 but has since been redeveloped. (Neil Davenport)

Brand new Leyland Titans, headed by T44, line up at the Aldenham Works Open Day on 16 September 1979. With input by LT into the design to ensure that, unlike their predecessors (Merlins, Swifts and Fleetlines) they were capable of withstanding London's demanding operating conditions (heavy traffic, closely spaced bus stops, etc), the Titan fleet, along with the contemporary Metrobuses, matched expectations and gave good service. T44 was bodied by Park Royal (the majority of the class of 1,125 plus five second-hand ones had Leyland bodies owing to the closure of Park Royal in November 1979) and entered service at North Street (Romford). The bus wears plain red livery, white upper window surrounds having been discontinued from T32 onwards. T44 was withdrawn in 1994 and headed north to Merseybus in Liverpool, later being resold and eventually cannibalised for spares followed by scrapping in September 2001. *(Bob Greenaway/Online Transport Archive)*

Almost new Leyland National LS 300, working route 108 (Stratford – Eltham) in September 1979 stands in Bromley High Street, Bromley-by-Bow, on the edge of the Bow Bridge Estate, a residential development started in the 1930s by the London County Council. The bridge is a reference to the crossing over the River Lea, now a flyover, which also spans the entrance to the Blackwall Tunnel. The 108 service, similar to the present one, originated in 1914 and may be remembered for the domed roofed (tunnel) STLs that used to operate through the Tunnel until it was altered in 1953, allowing standard buses to be used. The route today is reckoned to be the most unreliable in London owing to frequent traffic disruptions in and around the Blackwall Tunnel. LS 300 entered service at Poplar in June 1979, replacing Swifts, and was withdrawn at Fulwell in June 1990, whereupon it was sold for further service. *(John May/Online Transport Archive)*

LT operated a network of staff bus services between various towns and garages (including those later transferred to London Country) and the overhaul works at Aldenham and Chiswick. This was largely a legacy originating from a time when staff were transferred there from other locations, e.g. Fulwell, Charlton and Reigate, which had previously undertaken major overhaul work, or else moved to Hertfordshire to work on wartime aircraft manufacture at Aldenham. An assortment of different bus types was employed over the years but from February 1978 through to 1987, LT used ex-British Airways Routemasters, which it had purchased during the 1970s and designated RMAs. This view, dated 16 September 1979, shows a line up of RMA staff buses including, from right to left, RMA 14 – used on the Borehamwood run – and RMA 16, with a slipboard for Two Waters (Hemel Hempstead garage). RMA 14 is now preserved while RMA 16 was exported to Sweden in 1998 following use by Clydesdale Scottish and London & Country. (*Bob Greenaway/Online Transport Archive*)